THINK YOU'LL BE HAPPY. Copyright © 2023 by Nicole Avant. All rights reserved. Printed in the United States of America. No part of this book may be used or reproduced in any manner whatsoever without written permission except in the case of brief quotations embodied in critical articles and reviews. For information, address HarperCollins Publishers, 195 Broadway, New York, NY 10007.

HarperCollins books may be purchased for educational, business, or sales promotional use. For information, please email the Special Markets Department at SPsales@harpercollins.com.

FIRST EDITION

Designed by Bonni Leon-Berman

Unless otherwise noted, all photographs are courtesy of the author.

Library of Congress Cataloging-in-Publication Data has been applied for.

ISBN 978-0-06-330441-3

23 24 25 26 27 LBC 5 4 3 2 1

THINK YOU'LL BE HAPPY

MOVING THROUGH GRIEF
GRIT, GRACE, AND GRATI[

✦ ✦ ✦

NICOLE AVAN[

HarperOne

An Imprint of HarperCollinsPublishers

In the book you're about to read, you'll notice that references to my father, Clarence Avant, are in the present tense. Sadly, on Sunday, August 13, 2023, just as this book was going to press, my wonderful dad passed away. He was ninety-two.

We are devastated to have lost him. He was a titan, one of the greatest of Americans, a man who made a difference to so many lives . . . and he was also my dad, a mischievous, profane, loving, brilliant father. I can see him even now, sitting in the yard of my California home, listening to Ellington, or Sinatra, or my seventies playlist, and cursing at the size of the ravens in our garden. . . . But it seems appropriate that references to my father in this book remain in the present tense. Clarence *lives*; my mother, Jacqueline, *lives*; their lives were so extraordinary that to even conceive of them as in the past makes a mockery of time, let alone grammar. So, in the present tense he remains: Clarence Alexander Avant, 1931–2023. And boy, did he make something of the dash between those dates.

For my parents

• • •

Contents

Introduction

I was home alone on the evening of Tuesday, November 30, 2021. Well after midnight—I'd been asleep for hours by this point—something told me to look at my phone. When I did, I saw something you never want to see in the middle of the night: about a million missed calls from my brother, Alex, and the same from my husband, Ted, who was close by at a work retreat. With my heart racing, before I could even work out what was going on, my husband's name appeared on the screen again. I quickly answered his call and before I was able to say hello, he said something to me that would change my life forever.

"Love, you've got to get up, get dressed, and get to Cedars—your mom's been shot."

Surrounded by the darkness of night, I froze. "This is a dream," I thought. "This isn't happening. I just have to wake up. Wake up, Nicole. It's a nightmare. Wake up."

There are some words that make no sense and will never make any sense. Never, never, never.

"What the hell are you talking about?" I said. "Where was she? Was she out with my father? Wait, what time is it?"

Yet even as I asked, I realized quickly that there was no time for questions. I needed to go to my mother.

+ + +

My mother, Jacqueline, was the person in our family who held the pieces together when things were about to fall apart. She never stood on the sidelines. Like the queen of a kingdom, in moments of crisis her instinct was to act. For my entire life I saw her deliberately move through the world with grit, grace, and gratitude.

In that moment after I received the call, I left myself. Maybe I became my mother or maybe I became more deeply myself. I am not sure, but what I do know is that my mother needed a woman like her right then. I had no idea how shattered our lives would be, but I knew that as my mother's daughter, I had to hold the pieces together. There was no time to wonder, to parse meaning. I learned from both my parents that when there was a challenge, sitting still until a solution wandered by wasn't good enough.

Nothing good ever happens by sitting on a damn couch.

So I brushed my teeth, got dressed. I went downstairs, put some food out for the dogs, and got in the car . . . calmly.

Not shaking. I could feel my mother everywhere; she was guiding me, as she'd always done. I was tremendously grateful for her. I felt her grit filling me. I prayed for grace.

I found myself driving west on Sixth Street toward Cedars-Sinai Medical Center. All the lights were green. When the last light before I had to turn into the hospital started to flicker, I took this as a sign that my mom was trying to connect with me.

"Mom," I said out loud, "I'm on my way to the hospital. I have no real idea what happened, except that you're eighty-one years old and you've been shot. I don't know by whom, or where, or why, but I'm on my way. And everything is going to be okay, regardless of what happens. Mom, if you can hear me, I don't know what God's plan is, but don't feel that you have to come back and take care of Alex or Dad, because I'll do that. Mom, you've lived a great life. I've got it from here."

She didn't need to be next to me to hear me.

I knew she received my message. I had no idea what state she was in, but I wanted to offer my strong, elegant mother the relief she deserved.

I felt the urge to compose myself, not because I was okay. I was not okay. I collected myself because I was raised to believe that love is an action word. Love is not only something we are. Love is something we do. Love, the act of love, like the series of green lights, was moving me forward, telling me to keep going.

When I arrived at the hospital, the first person I saw was my father. I looked down and noticed that his left sock was stained with blood. I was later told that the slippers he was wearing were brought to him by a neighbor who'd seen my father, in shock, without shoes, being questioned by the police on the street in front of his home.

Of all I witnessed and went through that night, the gesture of those slippers stays in my memory. We must never underestimate the impact of a simple act of care.

The next person I saw was my brother, Alex, frantically pacing around the room and on the phone, his girlfriend, Airess, at his side.

Soon, Ted arrived and the police told us what they knew about the night.

An intruder had broken into my parents' home at around 2:25 a.m. and while attempting to rob their home, had shot my mother in the back with an assault rifle.

My blood boiled. My heart felt as if it would leap through my chest. My deep sadness and fear were instantly covered with a blanket of anger.

Someone hurt my mother?

I couldn't comprehend it. How could anyone hurt my mother? A woman who lived with such respect for life. She wouldn't harm an insect. Believe me, I grew up witnessing my mother releasing various insects from inside her home back outdoors to where they belong.

Someone hurt my mother?

Hot, painful tears streamed down my face.

And then I looked up and saw my father, the man who'd spent his entire life living in the warmth of my mother's light. A light that was fading fast.

I felt myself coming apart, but I couldn't, for the sake of my family. At least not in this moment.

I took a deep breath. And I held the pieces.

When the surgeon appeared, I saw the look on his face and knew. We all knew.

My father always says, "You come with a number, and you end with a number."

Those are my mother's numbers, and this book is the dash in between:

Jacqueline Avant, March 6, 1940–December 1, 2021.

+ + +

The trauma of my mother's death is not the story of her life. Her ending was tragic, yes, but her life was beautiful. One of her great superpowers was her ability to acknowledge hardship without staying in it for too long. She never let anyone rob her of her faith in God and all the blessings bestowed upon her and our family.

I didn't realize how deeply her way of being was ingrained in me until she was taken from me. Even on my hardest days (of which I have had countless), I saw and felt my blessings. In the midst of my emotional devastation, I have found small moments of relief—the sun on my face, the flowers emerging in my garden at my home after the long winter, standing over the stove with my father making our morning eggs, my husband's humor, long and rewarding conversations with our children, afternoons on the couch with our dogs.

I am so thankful to my mother for teaching me to love what there is to love and hold on to what there is to hold on to, no matter what.

* * *

If you only glance at my mom's life, it could appear to be all glitz and glamour. She was always fashionable and perfectly put together—you would never see Jacqueline Avant in the world with even one hair out of place.

But if you take a deeper look at my mother—past the Chanel suit, the lipstick, the jaw-dropping jewelry—you'll find she was kind of a nerd. That is actually one of my favorite things about her.

She was born in Jamaica, Queens, New York, in 1940. She was a writer, an editor, and a voracious reader. Her first job was in New York City as a hospital technician and phlebotomist.

Maya Angelou said, "Each of us has that right, that possibility, to invent ourselves daily. If a person does not invent herself, she will be invented. So, to be bodacious enough to invent ourselves is wise." My mother was brave enough to invent and reinvent herself throughout her life.

She met my father in the early 1960s while auditioning for the Ebony Fashion Fair, a traveling benefit that consisted of the most beautiful Black women in America modeling clothing from the best designers in the world. Once they moved to California, she became the most stylish woman and philanthropist in Beverly Hills. I was born in 1968; Alex, my brother, arrived in 1971.

Even with that sheen of glamour, our family was and is Black with a capital *B*. A Black couple with a baby on the way moving into Beverly Hills in the midst of housing discrimination and redlining was hard to imagine back then. Los Angeles may have been overflowing with movie stars, athletes, hippies, artists, celebrities, and progressive industry leaders, but it was no less segregated than parts of the American South.

When we moved in, we had the Slotkin family on one

side and the Maltz family on the other. On our very first day, Mrs. Slotkin said to my mom, "*They* weren't very welcoming to us, either, but I would like to welcome you to the neighborhood."

Florence Slotkin showed my mom the ropes and became one of her best friends. She introduced my mom to the best parks to take me to in my stroller, restaurants in the neighborhood, grocery stores, dry cleaners, you name it.

I often feel that my mom's life really began in Los Angeles. Her roots were in New York, but her fruits came to bear in California. It is where she started her family and found her people. History and community were everything to my mother. Besides her faith, that is what she valued most.

Grief comes in waves, and in the moments when I feel like I am underwater, I find solace in this thought: my mother loved and was loved in return.

In this book I share how my mother's life experiences became my life lessons. I share the unexpected pathways and light-bulb moments I have found as I moved through my grief. I share stories of those who loved me through the most traumatic time of my life, and tales from the tribe of my parents' closest friends who raised and inspired me to be the woman I am today.

This book is a collection of memories, reflections, and thoughts that fueled me to keep going, and keep giving.

ONE

Think You'll Be Happy

—Your sweet potato pie is waiting for you. 😄
—Hi mom. Sorry I missed you earlier. Dad said you were resting. I was just telling Ted that I think our time expired on the pie. 😄 I'll see how I feel about it tomorrow. Have a good evening. 😊
—OK. Think you'll be happy.

Texts between my mom and me, November 30, 2021

My mom was a homemaker, but I don't mean that she was passive. She turned our home into an ecosystem where anyone—from an artist to a politician to a business leader—could feel warmth, soul, and connection.

My dad, Clarence, is funny and smart and can move around the world, but he's not a particularly social person and never used to take good care of himself. My mom was his lifeline—she kept him social and active.

My mother had this ability to make everyone rise to the occasion and show up as their best selves. If you wanted to be in the Avant home, you had to have a high vibration— she didn't care if you were famous or not, you were not coming into her home with negativity.

I didn't always welcome her close attention. I often felt that my mom hovered over me. Some people do so to protect those they love from life. For her, it was about guiding me to serve and know my power in any situation. She urged me to be unafraid in uncomfortable situations so that later in life I'd know how to thrive and survive instead of whine and complain. (But believe me, most of my life I was saying under my breath, "Land, woman, land! The hovering can stop!")

Today, I realize she "hovered" to remain close to me; she wanted me to be strong and clear and ready to hold the baton on the day it would be passed to me.

But what are you supposed to do when the baton lands in your hands on the heels of shock and tragedy?

◆ ◆ ◆

Neither my mother nor I knew that her last text to me would be the words "Think you'll be happy," but it is fitting that she left me with a mantra for resiliency.

My mother chose to live a victorious life. My mother believed that service was the most thorough way to share her blessings, rather than hoard them (she would say, "Blessings don't belong to us—they are only loaned").

She found joy in surrounding herself with beauty, too, cultivating an astonishing collection of Japanese lacquers, as well as works by prominent African American artists.

She chose to be happy regardless of the circumstances around her. That's who she was. It was all a choice. She knew that choosing to be happy begins with believing you will be happy. She always believed that things would get better. Mom understood that she was on display because of her position in life. She always made sure to have her "face on," and a smile. Her attitude was "If I've been blessed to play the role of Jacquie Avant in this lifetime then damn it, I'm going to show up as the most glorious version of myself that I can possibly be."

Blessings don't belong to us— they are only loaned.

My mom knew how to be warm and open without taking shit from people—including her own kids and husband!

My father, the legendary Clarence Avant, is the man behind so many brilliant music industry careers—Bill Withers, Lalo Schifrin, Jimmy Smith, Dinah Washington, Freda Payne, Don Cornelius, Andre Harrell, Jimmy Jam and Terry Lewis,

L.A. Reid and Babyface. A man who pulled himself out of Jim Crow–era poverty and racism until he became a king-maker in the entertainment business and used that power to move into sports, influencing the careers of Muhammad Ali, Jim Brown, Jackie Robinson, and Hank Aaron. Dad was able to say, without a hint of irony, "I don't have problems, I have friends."

He also had Jacquie.

One of my favorite stories about her was the night that Bill Withers and my father were butting heads before Bill's show at Carnegie Hall in New York City. These moments of friction were typical of those between artist and record executive, but on this particular night my father decided to be more annoyed than usual and announced he wasn't going to attend the concert at all. My mother let him huff and puff like a child, and then very calmly she said, "You are getting dressed and you are going to the show and you are going to fix things with Bill."

That night, from the stage, Bill looked out at the audience and said, "Is Clarence Avant in the house?"

My mother looked at my father and said, "See, how would you have felt if you hadn't been here? Like a fool, that's how!"

My mother wanted to help my father leave his anger and frustration so he could embrace joy and his duty to the work at hand. This is a lesson that my father would not always remember, but it's one that I have never forgotten. And it has saved me many times from wallowing for too long.

And it wasn't just Clarence she schooled.

My mother saved every award, trophy, flag, and commendation I ever received. One year, when I was around eight years old, I realized that I was not, after all, going to come in first, second, or third in my tennis camp class. I'd had dreams of being Evonne Goolagong, but I played more like Evonne *Move-Along*. I ran home one night and complained to my mother about it.

"There's only one thing to do," she said.

With that, she went out to the carport, moved her silver Cadillac Seville out onto the street, handed me a tennis racket and a ball, and said, "You're going to hit that ball against the carport wall over and over until you get better."

On the final day of tennis camp, sure enough I didn't come even close to the medals . . . until finally they announced, "Most Improved Player: Nicole Avant."

I couldn't believe my ears; I didn't even know such an award existed. To her final days, my mother always claimed that the two moments she was most proud of me in her entire life were the day I signed the papers at the State Department to become a United States ambassador, and the afternoon in 1977 when I got the "Most Improved" award in tennis.

◆ ◆ ◆

I carry two things with me that were left to me by each of my grandmothers after they passed—their Bibles.

My dad's mom was very open about her faith, though it still manages to cause some confusion at home. I always thought she was a Baptist; my dad says she was a Methodist. The great thing is, it doesn't matter. She set the tone for our entire family, and whatever creed she did or did not follow, what mattered was that she taught me to have a personal relationship with Jesus and to be led by his example. She would say to me, "You should just talk to him like he's your friend. Don't ask; just talk." To her, the whole reason for religion was to gain character, to be more like God (that is, good). If you're in it for anything else, then you're in it for the wrong reasons. So if your religion tells you to hurt people, or to blow up buildings, or to attack an abortion center, or to deny the rights of women or gay people or whoever doesn't look or sound like you, then here's a question: "Would God do this?" And if the answer is no, then the message isn't from him, and you shouldn't do that task in his name. In fact, you shouldn't do it, period.

I thank God that my grandmother taught me so early about the magic of the Divine. For her, it was always about character, *good* character. She would also say, "You have to *be* the blessing." So whether you were born into riches or poverty, into a joyful family or a broken one—you, me, all of us: we're called to be a blessing to those around us.

I don't take for granted anything I have achieved in my life as a Black American woman. And I recognize my unique upbringing. I am lucky and I am blessed. I was taught to honor our past and pay forward our fruits. My parents may have raised me in the bubble of Beverly Hills, but they made sure that bubble was not the lens through which I saw the world.

They made sure I always understood that after hundreds of years of erasure, abuse, and belittlement, even the most high-achieving Black people in all areas of life—business, sports, industry, the arts, science, you name it—have to work twice as hard for recognition.

The zip code of my birth was 90210, but my true background lay in North Carolina and Virginia, the birthplace of my parents and of our families of origin, and places where a strange fruit too often grew. I am a product of four centuries of bonds. My people endured literal bondage.

That is why I take my freedom so seriously. I want to do *real* work, effect *real* change. I want to do what I do driven by a faith in God and an emphasis on love, and by *seeing* people, and sharing stories, and getting involved—whether that is telling the stories of Black figures like my father, or the 6888, the first and only majority-Black, all-female World War II battalion. My parents taught me that faith and freedom are about moving toward the light and bringing everyone you possibly can into the light at all times. It is not work that is done in the darkness of the shadows.

My people prayed; damn, they prayed hard. That's why I pray hard now. They shouted their field hollers until they turned those hollers into jubilees, and on into the blues, and from the blues into R&B. But it all started from the seed of prayer.

That's why Bill Withers's song "Grandma's Hands" has always been one of my favorites—"Grandma's hands used to ache sometimes and swell. . . . Put yourself in Jesus' hands." He knew his history began on Sunday mornings. It began with God. That's why I keep my grandmothers' Bibles close.

A few days after I lost my mother, I sent my dear friend Amy to my childhood home and asked that she bring me my mother's Bible.

✦ ✦ ✦

The first prayer my mother made me memorize was Philippians 1:11: "May you always be doing those good, kind things that show you are a child of God, for this will bring much praise and glory to the Lord" (The Living Bible).

This prayer became my starting point as I created a road-map for grief. My friend Penny says, "Grief is the receipt from the universe showing that you loved someone or something and loved them very deeply."

I often think about what my mother would have done if what happened to us had happened to someone in her life. I sincerely believe she would have grabbed us all by the lapels, set us upright, and told us to create love out of hate, peace out of violence, just as my friends did for me. And she would have insisted we turn to God, too, to reflect and share his unending love and give him glory.

As for me, well, I've decided to make the pain count—and count for something *good*. It's not just my mother's example inspiring me: I am here on the shoulders of so many before me. Those great men and women who lived in terror every day, and for hundreds of years, and fought and prayed and believed enough for me to be writing this and speaking to you as a free person.

I'd face my grief by *doing*, by doubling down on faith, love, and my family.

My friend Jennifer reminded me that no one could possibly know what I was feeling or going through, and accordingly they had no right to tell me how to grieve or "start living again." "Go to this therapist." "Go to this doctor." "Go to this healer." "Call this support group." So often someone would dish out advice. And each time, Jennifer would very sternly remind me that I was on a path of my own—a path that no one would ever be able to comprehend because it was mine and mine alone. It wasn't my responsibility to explain my new life or my feelings to anyone. The grace Jennifer showed me in her words gave me the strength and the permission to bow out gracefully when necessary and without explanation.

Some people have asked if I am okay. I think I hate this question more than any other, because everyone already knows the answer: "No, I'm *not* okay—someone just killed my mother." I had a lot of people needing and wanting my attention constantly, and it made me feel as if I were failing them in some way. I'd think, "Could you maybe realize that I'm in the middle of an investigation? Maybe I'm taking care of a ninety-one-year-old? Maybe I'm trying to figure out what to write on my mother's tombstone?"

This has been the worst part of this process—when people have made my loss about *their* grief, *their* trauma, *their* sadness. So many people have wanted to know the details of that night and expected me to explain how such a horrific thing could happen to my family. "Why *not* my family?" is how I'd respond in my head. "Who are we that this *couldn't* happen to us?" One of life's most heartbreaking truths is that bad things happen to good people all the time. I was so uncomfortable being asked to answer questions as if I was a news anchor reporting a story rather than a daughter grieving the loss of her mother.

> Grief is the receipt from the universe showing that you loved someone or something and loved them very deeply.

Hope is an aggressively positive frame of mind, and I choose to be anchored in it. I've decided to expect something good every day, just as my mom found hope and goodness everywhere she looked (because she looked!). My faith is holding my head above these troubled waters, too—the joy of the Lord is my strength, and without joy, you can't actualize strength. Joy makes us stronger.

If you don't know the answer to life's most difficult questions, why always pick the worst possible option? Or as the great sage, my husband, Ted Sarandos, once put it to me, "Sometimes you just don't get to know the answer, Nicole. Your job is to trust and have faith in the Lord— that's all you can really do."

When he said that to me about my mom, I snapped. "How dare you tell me I don't get to know why, Ted? Someone has to *explain* this to me."

In some ways, that's the worst part of it: you know that there's no explanation coming.

So, with all the things I don't know—and they are legion—I'm choosing to follow the lead of goodness, of God, of Jesus—the first social activist. Of Buddha, Allah, Krishna. Of JFK, RFK, Malcolm X, Dr. Martin Luther King Jr., Medgar Evers, Frederick Douglass. Of Ida B. Wells, Shirley Chisholm, Ruby Bridges, James Baldwin. Of Booker T. Washington. Of Mother Teresa.

Of Jacqueline Avant.

In the face of terrible things, my mother would have said, "Think you'll be happy," just as she did to me in her last text. So I think I will be happy; I want readers also to be happy, to keep going, to find gratitude, and hold on to blessings.

* * *

I've realized a lot of things since my mother died. For a start, quitting is not an option. Doesn't matter how rough the seas are, you can't just jump ship. There are too many people I still love on the boat. Sadness comes in waves, but as the Buddha says, misery and suffering are often a choice.

I've seen the worst our world has to offer, and it happened to the best our world has to offer.

I've learned that forgiveness is an act of casting the burdens—burdens of humiliation, shame, blame, anger, disappointment, and hatred—back to the Divine. I don't condone what happened; that's not what forgiveness is. Instead, I'm working to give up the negative energy surrounding it. I do not want to be poisoned by it. There is a person in the world who took life from my mother, but that kind of energy won't take my life too.

I don't want to carry the sadness and anger I have toward the man who did this to my mother, so I'm casting my burdens upon God and choosing a different way: I'm worshiping God amid the worst storm imaginable.

JACQUELINE AVANT

"Grace is one of those things you can't predict. It doesn't just come, it shows up and blesses you. . . . That is how you always felt if you were in Jacquie Avant's presence. She showed up and you were blessed."
—OPRAH WINFREY

"She was the matriarch of our community. While I was not born and raised in LA, when I say 'our community,' I mean amongst Black people. But all other communities looked at her as a shining, living example of elegance. . . . With her, you realized you were talking to somebody deep. It wasn't a raindrop in a cup—it was more like standing next to the ocean."
—PHARRELL WILLIAMS

"Jacquie was the sweetest person you could ever meet. She had a beautiful soul, kind heart, and always had a kind word for everybody. She was quiet, yet powerful, and very smart."
—MAGIC JOHNSON

"Jacquie Avant was a wonderful woman, a great partner to Clarence and mother to Alex and Nicole, an active citizen, and a dear friend to Hillary and me for thirty years. She inspired admiration, respect, and affection in everyone who knew her. We are heartbroken. She will be deeply missed."

—BILL CLINTON

"I don't say this lightly, but a light has gone out in Los Angeles."

—FRED ROSEN, FORMER CEO OF TICKETMASTER

"I'm devastated and heartbroken by the loss of Jacquie Avant. She was an endlessly kind and generous soul who always sought out new ways to give back and lift others up."

—AL GORE

"My heart breaks for Clarence and Nicole and all the Avant family. This world can be so cruel and cold!! I have no idea what kind of subhuman could shoot an eighty-one-year-old woman, and in her own home. But you can rest assured that every available resource will be used to find whoever is responsible for this awful nightmare. This is tremendously sad."

—TYLER PERRY

TWO

Mom

*Your mom was one of the most special
and beautiful people (inside and out).
[She] raised all of us.*

On October 30, 2021, just about one month before we lost my mother, Lionel Richie was slated to induct my father into the Rock & Roll Hall of Fame. (When we were kids and hits would play on the radio, we'd never mention the artist—it was always the record label honchos: "That's Jerry's song," we'd say, or "That's Irving's song." "That's Geffen's song." "That's Berry's song." "That's Clive's song." "That's Dad's song." But please note: Lionel Richie was the one who always got full credit!)

Dad was to receive the Ahmet Ertegun Award, named after the famed Turkish American songwriter, entrepreneur, and cofounder of Atlantic Records. The award is given to "non-performing industry professionals who, through their dedicated belief and support of artists and their music, have had a major influence on the creative development and growth of rock & roll and music that has impacted youth culture." This was a very significant moment in my father's life: after all he'd done to champion the artistic lives of so many, now the musical establishment was finally and formally recognizing his contribution.

But then something else very significant happened. My mom made it clear to me that she wasn't going to attend the event. This was so unlike her that I was puzzled. She said that she didn't want to travel to Cleveland, where the Hall of Fame is, and it was COVID time . . . but looking back, I think something really important was happening in her heart.

"I'm tired," she told me, "and I haven't had a weekend to myself in over fifty years. You can deal with your father for two days. Good luck!"

That sat fine with me. I not only understood it but deeply respected it. But now, in retrospect, I wonder, Did she know she didn't have long and wanted a weekend to prepare her soul? She and my father believed deeply in intuition, in the mind telling you things, leading you places. I'll never know; but nothing could ever surprise me about my mother and what she knew of life.

◆ ◆ ◆

On Tuesday, March 3, 2020—just a few days before the world went to hell in a handbasket thanks to COVID-19—I attended a memorial service for Joe Smith, a man I deeply loved. If you're a fan of Van Morrison, James Taylor, Neil Young, Joni Mitchell, Fleetwood Mac, Randy Newman, the Grateful Dead, America, the Eagles, Frank Sinatra, Paul McCartney, Brian Wilson, Linda Ronstadt, Garth Brooks, Maurice White, Neil Diamond, Alice Cooper, Bonnie Raitt, or even Liberace, chances are you would have loved him, too.

Joe was a record executive at Warner Brothers and a true hero in the music business, but to many others, and to me and my family, he was even more. Joe and his wife, Donnie, were close family friends for over fifty years, and I have very fond memories of spending time at their home, where I often maneuvered myself close to Donnie's candy jar.

But on one of the visits to Joe and Donnie's house—this was when I was just a kid—I was made to sit in the car and wait. This was unusual, because I always went into the house and straight for the candy. But that day, my mom was noticeably off—she wasn't her usual serene, smiling self, and we'd driven to the Smiths in silence. Usually we'd have had the radio blaring, but that day nothing, and you could have cut the heaviness with a knife.

At the Smith house, I waited what seemed like forever, but eventually my mom got back in the car to drive us home. Now the atmosphere was even worse: there were tears rolling down Mom's face.

It was clear that she was lost in a deep, deep sadness. The pain was written all over my mom's face on that car ride home and I shared in the pain even though I didn't understand what was going on.

Much, much later, I would come to find out that this was the day that my mom begged Joe for his financial help to get us out of debt and save us. And it wasn't merely our house that was up for grabs—my mother was facing having to save her marriage as well as our friendships (my brother's and mine), our schooling, all our settled lives, as much as her own. She would have done anything to save us from that trauma. She knew that even to move to a state that had lower taxes and a more affordable standard of living, she'd have to borrow money before she could get us all on a plane to go live with our grandmother or whoever would have us. My father's businesses had failed, and our finances had gone to zero—below zero, in fact. So Mom took it upon herself to ask for help from their dear friends. With the folding of my father's other business endeavors, people whom I had grown to know and love were no longer to be a constant in my life, and this was my first experience with the feelings that grief brings. I saw that same pain later when Bill Withers and my father fell out. That breakup affected all of us. Bill was like a son to my father and like a brother to my mom. We were all heartbroken with our new reality—we were no longer the same.

Because of the extraordinary kindness of friends, eventually my father was able to dust himself off and start over; a few years later, he established the legendary R+B label Tabu Records, and even rose to become the chairman of Motown Records.

In the decades from that eventful day until Joe's passing, my parents and the Smiths spent many nights out having dinner at the Tower Bar in Los Angeles, or the Polo Lounge in Beverly Hills, and Joe always made sure to bring the good wine!

This is what I love about them: they all chose to live life to its fullest and enjoy it as much as possible with good food, good wine, and good company. My mom always came home from those dinners happy and fulfilled because they'd spent their time reminiscing about the "good old days" and counting their blessings; all four of them realized that they'd been blessed with a magnificent life, through good and bad.

Now, in March 2020, I was at the memorial for Joe with my mother and father, who stoically held their grief back, even though they had just had their monthly dinner with Joe and Donnie weeks prior.

In a 1993 *Los Angeles Times* article, Joe was asked this question about his past: "In those days, what did it take to be a successful executive?"

His answer resonated for me when I read it three decades ago, and it resonates still: "Well," Joe said, "it took a lot of energy. Because your energy was immediately reflected in your enthusiasm." I couldn't agree more. We all have a choice when it comes to our energy.

Since the loss of my mother, lots of people have said to me, "I can't imagine how you feel." It's just something people say. My answer is, Imagine this: I have a choice. I either let what happened to my mother define me and rule my life, or I choose something else. I choose to work with energy, every day, and try to focus on being victorious versus being a victim. Every time I find myself slipping into victim mode, I declare, "No! I choose victory." And that choice of victory is, as for Joe Smith before me, reflected in my enthusiasm. I choose to throw myself into my work, my family, my advocacy—all the things that matter to me—with renewed enthusiasm. Sadly, my mother is now one of my "ancestors," and like those ancestors, she remains an indelible force in my life every day. There are moments she's even more alive now than ever.

That day of the Joe Smith memorial, everybody was there—and it was wonderful to see one of my mom's dearest friends, Sandra Moss. The two women had been close friends for over fifty years. Jerry and Sandy Moss were staples in my childhood, and I often spent time with them at their home in Malibu. Those special days are etched in my mind. The ocean spoke to me; it was there by the water that I realized how vast our universe is. My mind was young, but it was open and in awe of every sunrise and sunset. The sound of the waves, the sweep of the birds, and the frolicking of the dolphins—all of it added up to something elemental. I used to exclaim, "I can't get over the fact that there's so much beautiful life in the ocean! Yet we can't interchange our realities!"

The adults would look at me with a mixture of amusement and confusion, but I knew what I meant. I was in awe of life and its grandness, and all I wanted to do was show up in this magnificence and be one with it.

The music blaring through the house didn't hurt either. Listening over and over to the A&M Records hits, interspersed with the Bill Withers hits from Sussex Records, was how I learned about life, death, love, friendship, loss, heartbreak, and fragility. So much of what I learned about life, I learned from a song.

I told Ted after Joe Smith's memorial that everybody in that room had raised me. If I acted up at someone's house, they didn't wait to tell my mom three hours later; they corrected me in the moment. They asked my friends and me questions about the world and how we saw it and how we saw our future selves. We mattered to them as *people*, not just as someone's kids.

Mom and Sandy empowered us constantly, too. They didn't lecture; they just reminded us that they, too, were fabulous and strong and powerful and creative. It wasn't just the men; the women knew how to create and strive and nurture and be successful. Sandy would hear one of us kids say, "We're gonna be so powerful—just like our dad," and she'd step right in.

"Honey," she'd say, "your mom and I are just as intelligent as these men! We're just as cool, just as creative. There were limitations put on us, but we pushed them down for you so that you could walk through the door. Yes, you've seen my modeling photos, you've seen your mother's modeling photos, and you probably think that's all that we wanted to do. But you're wrong, honey—that was the easiest thing that we could do. We wanted to do other things, but there you are. Now you're giving all this credit to these men, but hello? We're just as smart! And one last thing, honey—now that we've opened the door for you, you better walk through it!" That lesson has stayed with me throughout my life.

In the fall of 2021, years after that conversation, we sadly attended Sandy's memorial service. This woman who had helped raise me had had the long view, a sense of a lived life as part of a long tradition, not simply a single span. As evidence of that long view, she had recognized that a memorial service delayed a year had more of a chance of being a celebration than a dirge—and she had planned accordingly for her own. The memorial service was held in September, on what would have been her birthday, one year after her death, and a Thanksgiving menu was served—it was her favorite food—and there was a photo montage and music and stories and laughter. The memorial was intensely positive. Sandy had thought to have her favorite cleric, Father John Bakus, a Greek Orthodox priest and the dean of Saint Sophia Cathedral in LA, memorialize her life.

After he finished speaking, my mother turned to me and said, "I want him to do my memorial," to which I replied, "You're basically a Buddhist now, so I doubt he'll be speaking at your funeral."

Fast-forward to December 17, 2021, and the tiny funeral service we held for my mother (COVID-19 had reared its ugly head again). Sure enough, there was Father Bakus memorializing my mother.

That day we all sat in the front row—Ted and I, Dad, and Alex. Alex and I had Dad wedged between us. I noticed that my brother was trembling.

During the service, as we listened to Father Bakus eulogize my mother, my dad suddenly grew very calm. Then he grabbed my hand and Alex's hand. I think this was the first time he'd truly acknowledged that his children's mother had died.

Instantly, I was taken back to memories of the bike store we loved to visit on Beverly Boulevard when we were kids. To get there, we'd jaywalk across the street, Dad holding our hands to make sure we were safe. That was the last time I could remember him holding my hand. Right there, in that church that day of my mother's memorial, the delightful smell of a bike store—a heady mixture of oil and rubber and metal—seemed to fill those old pews. Like incense, it imparted holiness. After all, everyone loves the smell of a bike store, because only good things happen there—your first bike, your first *real* bike, your first bike as an adult. Which color, which bell, which basket, which destination? The freedom of this simple machine, the deep, unmitigated joy of a brand-new bicycle, all those possibilities running through a young mind as each potential ride is hoisted down from its rack. Then the questions—"Can your feet reach the pedals?" *Yes!* "Do you like the color?" *Yes!*—and the dreamed of final words, just a few of them, simple but filled with all the promise of rides not yet taken as your father says, "We'll take it."

All these memories came to me that day as my father gripped my hand, decades on from Beverly Boulevard, so many years on from hope, on this, the darkest of days.

◆ ◆ ◆

My mentors were true activists and used their various platforms to open doors and lift people up. They took time to guide everyone coming up behind them. Their focus, integrity, intention, and perseverance set the standard for all of us following behind.

In the process, they created a soundtrack for my life: Joe Smith, Jerry Moss and Herb Alpert, Bill Withers, Quincy Jones, Don Cornelius, Berry Gordy, Smokey Robinson, Diana Ross, David Geffen, Irving Azoff, Clive Davis, Lionel Richie, Suzanne de Passe. I can't imagine what my life would have been like without their music to sustain and uplift me.

People like Joe Smith didn't just inspire me; they also supported me. If not for folks like Joe Smith and Jerry Moss—

both of whom stepped in to save my father from financial ruin at a crucial point in my childhood—everything would have been different for me and my family. We would have lost our home for starters, and who knows what else might have changed for the worse. Joe and Jerry proved that true friendship is not fair-weather only; it's built on a rock, not on quicksand. Both Joe and Jerry came from nothing, as did my father, and when they saw a need, they stepped in, remembering where they'd come from and how close we all are to having dust, not dollars, in our pockets. As 1 Corinthians 13:13 says: "And now abide faith, hope, love, these three; but the greatest of these is love."

On the morning of that fateful December 1, after news broke of my mother's death, I remember old friends of the family calling. Just hearing their voices gave me a sense of calm, and I knew that things would be okay down the line because I had a great support system that I could count on.

I also felt the river of care provided by friends of my own generation. Sure, some people said they couldn't imagine how I felt and left it at that, but many others stepped up. Like Joe and Jerry ministering to my parents years earlier, my friends recognized a need and threw themselves into helping me and my family; they brought their energy to bear on a situation that for many might have seemed unbearable. And they did so enthusiastically, even when faced with some of the terrible things they had to tackle in helping me (we'll get to that later).

The older generation that undergirds my support system—this is what I mean by ancestors. Yes, ancestors are those ancient faces peering out from faded, cracked photographs, but they are also the people in our lives who form our character, who bring the insights of a previous generation to us who are too young to know the real meaning of sacrifice and commitment. All too often we feel as though we know everything, an attitude personified in a college graduate starting a new job and wondering within weeks when the first raise and promotion will show up. But we're all apprentices in life; none of us knows enough to get by on our own. The great advantage we all have is that there are plenty of elders and ancestors from whom we can learn.

I stand on the shoulders of these people, the many who have paved the way for me, and now a cadre of incredible friends keep me afloat, each with their own insight and experience that I can draw on to strengthen my own character. We may feel like we're alone on this planet, but very few of us are truly without support. Yet even when we acknowledge our mentors, how many of us honor that network? It's not just a matter of taking things for granted; we all too often think we're fighting through this world alone, which leaves us feeling that all of our successes and triumphs are likewise ours alone.

We couldn't be more wrong. Nothing happens in a vacuum; we are all products of the people around us, borne along the troubled waters by acts of kindness. This community of care became strikingly apparent when my mother died; in fact, it reinvigorated me: I felt myself urged by that love to redouble my efforts to look outward, to live a life worth living.

Because you never know what's going to happen.

More than anything, we have grown tired, siloed, isolated; and I genuinely believe we all want to see the rise of community once again—community, and kindness, and a recommitment to learning from those who know better. Yes, my family and I went through the worst thing anyone might imagine, but what I found in the rubble of the weeks and months after my mother's death was a world filled with real community and genuine kindness, and I honor that world. I don't remember everything that people did, but people just showed up, each with a different gift. Gwyneth was organizing everyone and everything. Danielle and Dora were cooking. Candace and Laura were finding my mom a resting place. Colleen and Juliet hopped on planes from Switzerland and Miami to come and be by my side.

We're all apprentices in life; none of us knows enough to get by on our own.

And even people who might not have shown up right away to give help quickly fell into step with the love and support of those around me.

Take Reed Hastings, for example. Reed cofounded Netflix; he is many incredible things, but one thing I'm pretty sure he wouldn't admit to is being a regular attendee of prayer circles.

And yet in December 2021, he really didn't have a choice.

My friend Cleo brought her gifts to bear many times and in many ways after my mother died. One of the ways was to lead a prayer circle in my home. One evening, Reed showed up looking for Ted. Some of my girlfriends and I were getting ready to be led in prayer by Cleo in the kitchen—which she had filled with candles, incense, crystals, and photos of various divine beings and angels.

Cleo is from New Orleans. Explains it all, right?

"Oh, hey guys," Reed said, looking a little confused. "I was looking for Ted."

"He's in the other room with my dad," I said.

"We're about to start, Reed," Cleo said, invitation in her voice.

There was a pause. Reed could either make his excuses—that would have been totally fine!—or he could bring his energy to us.

He didn't hesitate. Without fanfare, Reed Hastings huddled with a bunch of women as Cleo began her incantation.

He said all the amens, too. This is what I mean by community and kindness. Praying with us might not have been directly in Reed's comfort zone, but discomfort didn't stop him from getting involved in an incredibly meaningful way.

Sometimes, all it takes is showing up.

✦ ✦ ✦

We are all products of long histories, and we are called to honor the legacy of our ancestors and build upon the lessons they taught us—in other words, to step up when called. We cannot simply coast on the gains they made for us, nor can we waste the love that people bring at our darkest moments.

I know I was lucky to have such a wide range of incredible people around me as a child and a younger woman. At Joe Smith's memorial, I knew that we weren't honoring just the man; we were also honoring the legacy that he'd created, the wisdom he'd shared, the love he'd so generously given not only to my parents in their hour of need but to so many others (heck, he signed Bonnie Raitt on two separate occasions!). There was no question what Joe and others showed me in every interaction: they raised everyone around them to serve . . . and it wasn't just some kind of dry example, either; they were out there on the front lines of service.

When we weren't being shown by them how to serve,

we were being taught to honor and ingest as much culture as possible. It seems crazy to me that art is thought of as elitist—because for my parents and their friends, culture and the arts were everything. A love of and involvement in the arts was the surest sign that someone had risen from their poverty-stricken beginnings into a place where the mind could be cultivated and educated and refined.

I think about much harder times than the ones in which we currently live: the Great Depression, for example. As part of the relief for struggling Americans, the New Deal focused some of its efforts on the arts. Sure, the Works Progress Administration may have been responsible for beautiful bridges and roads and buildings, but a significant part of the program was given over to artists, to make paintings, sculptures, murals, photographs—you name it. Under President Roosevelt, part of the WPA funding was given over to the Federal Art Project, which supported myriad efforts to shore up the artistic culture of our country. And this *mattered* to Americans. Accordingly, my mom grew up with the idea that the arts and culture were vitally important—after all, her president had said so and had funded their propagation—and *her* mother, too, believed in what FDR had to say. (Those were the days when a president was respected because he was the president, no matter the color of his campaign poster.) To

FDR, and to so many Americans rooted in his era, the arts were one of the most important things we have.

And a love of the arts wasn't just theoretical to my parents and their parents—sometimes to a young Nicole Avant's cost, I might add. I still remember my thirteenth birthday party. I'd wanted to go roller-skating at Flipper's with a group of friends, as any thirteen-year-old Angeleno might. I didn't think it was that much to ask... until my dad had other ideas.

"Duke Ellington's *Sophisticated Ladies* is playing at the Shubert Theatre," he said, "so that's what you're doing for your birthday party. Gregory Hines is in it, and Duke's grandkid Mercedes, too. So you and your pals are going, end of conversation."

This wasn't bloody-mindedness on his part, though it might have felt that way to a thirteen-year-old. Instead, it was a reminder that when it came to honoring my culture, and culture generally, it was important to realize that I wasn't growing up in a vacuum. Roller-skating to "I'm Coming Out" by Diana Ross might have seemed like more fun, but the chance to hear the music of Sir Duke and witness the genius dancing of Gregory Hines? For my parents, there was no question which was more important, which would make me a better-educated person. And by *education* they didn't necessarily mean just ABCs—they meant becoming educated as to the world of my forebears and betters, those who'd had to struggle to improve themselves against all odds, who had committed their lives to creating great art despite the barriers. (Just think about Hines himself, who always described Sammy Davis Jr. as his most beloved mentor. When Davis was dying, Hines went to see him. As he was leaving, Hines recounts, Davis threw an imaginary ball to him, as if to pass on the older man's legacy. Such moments of ancestral transference aren't theoretical; they're tangible examples of the crucial continuity and power of community.)

I knew how lucky I was. When my father was a thirteen-year-old, he was kicked out of his house for defending his mother from his emotionally and physically abusive step-father and found himself alone, riding a train to New Jersey to escape his tough family background—no Shubert Theatre for him back then. When Duke Ellington was in the eighth grade, he was told that if he found himself next to a white woman in a theater, he was to behave his best because he was representing his race. My father didn't need to tell me that story to underline what Duke Ellington went through; he just made us listen to the music and skip roller-skating so that we, too, could be "sophisticated ladies." There was a whole world of struggle and a lack of opportunity that I needed to know about and to use to fire my own future, because if you don't stand for something, you'll fall for anything.

Mom

It wasn't just my father who made sure I knew my history, cultural or otherwise. My mother was steeped in history, too—though the lessons she learned from history, and that she imparted to me, weren't always the ones you might imagine.

I remember one year we brought permission slips home because our school wanted to show us a movie about the death of John F. Kennedy, and some of the scenes would be potentially harrowing for kids. I was probably around ten years old, so this was the late seventies, and back then, parents were a bit different from how they are now—tougher perhaps, less helicopter-y, and certainly more willing to let their children be exposed to the realities of an often-cruel world. There were maybe two kids in my class who weren't allowed to watch the movie (I dread to think how many would be kept away now), but I remember how fervently my parents wanted me to see it, especially my mom.

The movie itself made a huge impression on me. I remember going home and running in to see my mother in our living room.

"I can't believe how Jackie O tried to grab the remains of JFK's brain!" I exclaimed, before I'd even said hello. That moment, to me, was the most incredible one of the whole film—to love someone so much that you'd do something so unfathomable. "I can't believe this happened," I added, which is something I always seemed to say about the history I was learning.

My mother saw it differently. "Nicole," she said, "you have it all wrong."

I was confused. "But Mom, she actually tried to save parts of his brain."

"Instead of being in disbelief, Nicole, or focusing on the gruesome details of the tragedy, you need to say, 'I can't believe all these great things these people did. I can't believe the way they lived for other people. I can't believe that they got up every day to serve.'"

That was why my mother had signed the permission slip in the first place—not so her daughter could be horrified by an assassination, but rather so that she could learn the lessons of the life lived by whatever person was involved, be it President Lincoln, JFK, RFK, or Martin Luther King Jr. The incidentals of their death were just that—incidental. What mattered was the life they'd lived.

If you don't stand for something, you'll fall for anything.

I would think about this lesson—that *life* is what matters, not the manner of a death—many times in the months after my mother's passing. It gave me great comfort, and still does. My mother understood that no one knows how life will end, no one knows what or how long a future is, so the only thing to do is to live fully, to expand one's horizons as long as one has breath to do so.

And when someone is gone, to focus on the good, not the loss.

* * *

One of my mom's favorite sayings was "You have a choice: sink or swim." Back then, I didn't really get it—I was just a kid trying to have as much fun as possible. But she saw greater things for me, for all of us. My mother wanted the history I studied to leap off the page, to instill in me the fire to do stuff—shut up, get up, and do stuff—not sink, but swim.

In her early twenties, my mother had admired Andrew Goodman, a young man who, along with James Chaney and Michael Schwerner, was murdered by the KKK in Mississippi in 1964, during the Freedom Summer of the civil rights era. Goodman, Schwerner, and Chaney were in Mississippi to help register Black Americans to vote. They were abducted in Neshoba County, in the central part of the state, and each shot to death. (Their deaths would form the basis of the movie *Mississippi Burning* many years later.)

My mom was just twenty-four when that tragedy happened,

doing volunteer work in Queens, New York. These young men were her same age, give or take a year or two. They, too, had wanted to do good, to spread love, to be a good American; had wanted to fight for someone else's rights. They went down to Mississippi, and they never came back.

My mom said, "When we found out they were killed, it changed everything. It was so real to me; Andrew could have been me. First, it made me stop in fear. Then it made me angry. Then it made me sad. And then, once I'd cried it out, I knew I had to get back up, because the only way I could really honor Andrew was to go out and do things for people."

JFK had told young people to volunteer and to serve ("Ask not what your country can do for you," etc.), and so many, like Goodman and like my mother, did so.

"He gave us something to do," she said later, referring to JFK. "He inspired us, but he also gave us a homework assignment: he told us to *serve*."

Like Goodman, my mother was a native New Yorker and was involved in the civil rights struggle. It's not an overstatement to say that Goodman's murder changed her life. History, for her, became something tangible, real, present; it was no longer the stuff of musty words in textbooks, of ancient figures speaking in stilted language, but a real, breathing, teaching element. And so it became for me, too—I had no choice! When I learned history, it wasn't so much that it made me smarter or helped me not repeat it. No, in my house growing up, history was much deeper than that. I found out who I wanted to be when I studied history. When I looked at Frederick Douglass or Harriet Tubman or Ida B. Wells or MLK, what stood out for me was that, through all the challenges, through all the hatred, through all the trauma, through all the unfairness, those individuals still completed their tasks, ran their races right through the finishing tape and beyond. The key to making change is to never stop moving forward. These women and men held that key: they never stopped moving forward.

Consider the Tuskegee Airmen, Black men who served with distinction in World War II. They lived under Jim Crow laws like all other Black folks. They weren't free men, far from it—they couldn't go into the hotels they wanted to or eat at the same lunch counters as white folks. They faced discrimination and prejudice at every turn. But they didn't give up, didn't just say screw this. Instead, they learned how to fly WWII airplanes, and their support staff worked out how to create a cogent and unassailable organization, and together this extraordinary group of people became one of the most decorated in the United States military.

What drove the Tuskegee Airmen to persist and excel, despite discrimination and prejudice? They never gave up because they could see the bigger purpose, and they understood that that purpose wasn't about them. When it's not only about you, you find the strength to continue moving forward. That's what I learned from history—to feel a responsibility, whether I change someone else's life or not. To at least run the best race that I can because somebody did it for me. This life isn't about me; it's about what I can give to other people. My job is to pass the baton on, just as it was thrust to me by my ancestors.

And that's what my mother did for me, above all else. She handed me the baton that she had been handed (by her forebears, by Andrew Goodman, by so many), and even though her death blurred my eyes with so many tears that some days it was hard to see the legacy, I couldn't help but feel it constantly. In fact, I feel it everywhere. That's history, her history, in me, through me, a river that cannot run dry.

◆ ◆ ◆

The day after Joe Smith's memorial, I found time to visit with another hugely crucial influence in my life, Quincy Jones.

Quincy is my godfather, and I probably spent more time in Quincy's house growing up than even in my own. (He and my father were, and still are, best friends.) Quincy, like so many others who taught me how to live a useful life, came from a hardscrabble childhood marked by privation and violence. A child of the Great Depression, Jones was stabbed in the hand at the age of seven when he mistakenly ended up on the wrong street, as he later put it, in the South Side of Chicago. Worse yet, his mother developed schizophrenia and was institutionalized, leaving him at the mercy of a stepmother who favored her own children over Quincy.

Surely it was not in his childhood mind that he'd one day be the most sought-after producer, composer, and conductor on the planet. He had to have seen something that could not be seen, something that drove him. He somehow knew that he had to make his life happen by being ready, and by persevering. His brother Richard, who went on to be a judge in Washington State, described what the kids called a "dream window" in their house in Seattle. "We weren't looking at a spectacular lake," Richard said, as quoted in *The Seattle Times*. "We grew up looking at the blackberry bushes and garbage in the lot across the street. You had to have a big imagination." Quincy Jones obviously did! And the greatest gift that he gave me is a belief in the power of my own imagination, along with the knowledge that what I do with that imagination is always my choice. Why not use it for the things that I want to experience instead of the things that I fear or that I don't want to do?

Quincy was always completely open and honest about his mom and was never ashamed of his upbringing. Nor was my father—Clarence Avant's stepdad used to beat the hell out of my grandmother in front of him, but Dad never laid the future of his life on that trauma. Instead, these men threw their lot in with a kind of synchronicity, an urgent belief that you could still be in the right place at the right time, despite what your upbringing had given you. Quincy could have been a gangster—he even once said he'd wanted to be one!—but then music changed his trajectory.

But it's not only a case of right place, right time—it's also about whether or not you are open to the blessing. And being open to the blessing is all about preparation. That's why, every single day, I pray that everything is in divine order; I ask for divine intelligence, for divine grace. Each morning, I start my day with this prayer: *Today is the day the Lord has made, and I choose to be glad and rejoice in it; I choose to trust that I will be aligned with whomever and whatever I'm supposed to be aligned with this day—and may I be a blessing.* That's it—I pray that I do the best I can, and I choose to be grateful for my life. I think about my father, trying to make his way, about my mother, about Quincy Jones. *All* of the great mentors in my life followed divine breadcrumbs, if you will. That's where I get my prayer from—in essence, I'm opening my imagination in order to follow the breadcrumbs that God is leaving for me.

Imagination is the greatest tool that human beings have. It's primarily what sets us apart from other animals, who don't have the power of choice fueled by imagining a different way to be. (As I always say, "Camels can't decide." No really,

I actually say that all the time!) Recently, I was having the most frustrating day—I was angry and annoyed, but quickly realized that the frustration was a good thing. Frustration is a disappointment alarm that signals that something's not working, something's not sitting right. This means we have to pivot; we have to dig into our imagination and find a way out of negative thoughts. Again, this was part of the legacy of men like Quincy and my father, who could easily have fallen prey to disappointment and inertia. Instead, they took every chance they could to change their world.

Quincy has lived a life of imagination, and I don't mean just as an artist. Quincy always wants to know about you, and he imagines the best for you. Another lesson he's taught me: if you care about people, always imagine the best-case scenario for them.

He has often said to me, "When you travel the world, keep your heart and your mind open. Be open to meeting new people and making new friends. Listen to their music, visit their museums, be curious about the environment you're in. After all, these are your brothers and sisters, just from a different mama."

My mother agreed. She believed in cultural appreciation and reminded me not to fall into the craziness of cultural appropriation—that's another thing she and Quincy gave me. That's why, when I had the chance to go to Russia in high school, the trip took on a mythical quality for Quincy and for his best friend, my father. They grilled me for months about it—but why did it matter so much to them?

When I asked Quincy about it recently, he said, "Nicole, not in a million years would your father or I ever have thought we'd be sitting in his house talking about his Black child going to the Soviet Union with her high-school class for Christmas break in 1985! It was unimaginable that your life could be so very different from our lives as Black teenage men in America in 1950. Different times, baby. Different times. That feeling of 'Can you believe the change that occurred for our children to have this new and better life?' has never left your dad and me."

You have to have boots on your feet in the first place to be able to pull yourself up by your bootstraps. I understand that term and use it a lot when referring to any type of laziness in anyone. But I'd argue that Black Americans have done better than pull up their bootstraps. Having faced slavery, Jim Crow, segregation, daily terrorism of bombs and dogs, bulldozers—every evil imaginable—we've still thrived. We've established more than forty historically Black colleges and universities, and we've delivered plentifully in medicine, science, sports, entertainment, business. All against the odds; all while facing down a culture that sometimes thinks of us as second-class citizens.

PHARRELL, THE BISHOP, AND EDDIE

A few days after my mother died, Pharrell Williams called. He's like a brother to me—he's family. "We're gonna celebrate your mom," he said. "We're gonna celebrate her legacy. She's a big deal. And we're not gonna let anyone forget her. She created a life worth talking about. Do you realize that hundreds of thousands of babies were born around the world the day she passed over? There are 140 million a year all around the world! Life is always continuing, Nicole, and you must continue her life by living yours to the fullest."

He concluded, "God is still the greatest." Pharrell says this all the time, through good or bad times, and he's right—God *is* still the greatest.

A short time after she died, I found myself in agony on my knees. At that very moment, my phone rang.

"Is this Nicole?" a voice said.

"Yes, who is this?

"This is Bishop Jakes."

I told him I was on my knees.

"Good," he said, "then we'll pray."

And we did.

After a while he said, "What are you angry about?"

"Well, obviously, I'm angry that that man broke in. I'm angry that he hurt my mom. He didn't have to shoot her. He could have just left. I'm angry that she had to be so brave as to not call my dad's name otherwise he might have been shot too. . . . I'm angry that in just five minutes everything changed."

"Are we gonna give this guy five minutes of your mom's life?" Bishop Jakes said. "Or are we going to focus on the eighty-one years of your mom's life? Can we give her that? It's your choice—you have free will. So, which is it?"

"The eighty-one years," I said, and then he proceeded to ask me every conceivable question about my mom.

Eventually, he said, "She lived a life, and your job is to celebrate it. And the way you celebrate her life is you honor her life. You talk about that life. You talk about all the good. You talk about the times she made you laugh. Keep talking like that and don't forget the lessons."

But much as I loved the support, something else happened that filled my heart to the brim.

My mom was the queen of Beverly Hills, of every supermarket, of every gas station. At one station, Eddie, the attendant, came running up to me. He pulled down his COVID mask and I saw that he was weeping.

"I filled your mom's tank every single week," Eddie sobbed. "She was always so kind; even when she seemed busy, she took time to talk to me, ask about my children, and I knew she really cared about the answers. She was so nice to me—she really saw me, every time she came by."

What that beautiful man at the gas station said about my mom is what Bishop Jakes meant; that's what Pharrell meant: we celebrate the people around us when we really see them, when we focus on the years not the minutes, when we let love be the lesson.

THREE

The Blessings of Our Ancestors

She was a role model to me. Over the years, every time my mom spent time with your mom she would tell me, now Jacquie is what everyone should aspire to be.

I grew up one generation away from Jim Crow and was the first in my family to be born with all my rights, but vestiges of that traumatic era remained everywhere I looked. Black people had spent hundreds of years in chattel slavery; unlike their white forebears, nothing had been given to them when they arrived. We had no farmland, no banks, no institutions. And the land we did own was often under threat of bulldozers or fires. So when my father's boss and greatest mentor, Joe Glaser, bought our house in Beverly Hills for us because my parents didn't have the money for the down payment and because it was just impossible to get a Realtor to turn up for a showing for a potential Black client, this was not just an extraordinary moment for one Black family; it echoed back through our shared history.

My dad had told Glaser he was looking for a house in Baldwin Hills, where most of the wealthy African Americans were living at the time. Joe Glaser had never heard of Baldwin Hills.

"What's wrong with Beverly Hills?" Glaser asked.

My father said, "I love it there—especially Trousdale Estates. My friend Abe took me to a party at Dinah Shore's house, and I said to Jacquie, 'If I ever make enough money and end up moving to California, I want to live here in Trousdale.' But I can't afford that."

Glaser said, "I didn't ask you if you could afford it." Glaser gave my father a loan, and my parents lived in that house for fifty-two years, until that fateful morning in 2021. In fact, the story of how my father got involved with Joe Glaser in the first place is another example of people using their imagination to improve the lives of those around them.

Joseph G. Glaser was a talent manager, mainly specializing in jazz musicians, including Louis Armstrong, running a shop called the Associated Booking Corporation. One day, Joe heard my father arguing with Dinah Washington—she was, according to my dad, "rough." By this point my father was managing the jazz organist Jimmy Smith and some other acts. Dinah, the legendary singer, was known for sometimes not paying her band, and my dad was arguing with her about that. Joe overheard their fight and laughed, but he then told Clarence Avant—a man who had grown up in Jim Crow's North Carolina—that he would make a great agent.

Now, it wasn't that Glaser was woke, or even especially ahead of his time, racially speaking—far from it. He didn't hang out with my dad all that much; they didn't eat at each other's houses regularly. But without Joe, I don't think my dad would have had much of a life. In fact, I don't know if he would've survived. Joe didn't just mentor my dad; he literally opened every single door for him. Everything that I do now as an adult, or that I have done, is passed on from my dad, but my dad got it from Joe, and Joe got it from the people who came before him. My dad would say, "Joe took me to the Yankee games and he never made me sit with the colored people. I would get ready to walk to the back, saying, 'I'm going to go sit with the colored people.' And Joe would say, 'No, you come sit here with me. We all shit the same way, Clarence—sit here and you'll learn things.'"

One of the most important things Joe Glaser passed on to my father, and he to me, was to simply sit and observe. A lot of Joe's teaching came down to that: sit in the room, listen to how we make the deals, and learn.

Glaser didn't wake up every day determined to make Black people's lives vastly better by focusing on Clarence. Instead, he saw somebody special, and he felt that he could make a difference in this young man's life. He saw someone who was willing to sit in the room, listen, and learn. These are such valuable traits in anyone, even now—*especially* now, in fact.

My father took Joe's mentorship into his own life—that's how my dad became known as the "Black godfather." He recognized his own power, and he knew he had the opportunity to open doors for the Black community. Not everyone was going to know what to do with the opportunity of an open door, but the advantaged had an obligation to step forward and open it. That's what my parents did, again and again.

Ironically, the man who killed my mother was the very kind of person she was working to help. That doesn't negate what she was doing; in fact, it makes her efforts—efforts we need to continue and amplify—that much more powerful and important. Because my mother's helpful deeds were done without the thought of where they would lead. They weren't deeds done with some reward in mind. They were done selflessly, and through love. That they were so cruelly betrayed in the cosmic scheme of things isn't the point; the ending doesn't negate the beginning and middle.

+ + +

The house Joe Glaser helped my parents buy was the one I grew up in, the one in which I got to spend time with all those extraordinary artists and thinkers—so much so that it developed a kind of aura around it. There is something very special about that house. (Sadly, a few years after he'd bought them the house, Joe Glaser died, and my father had no idea how he'd pay Glaser's estate back. And then a miracle happened. My father received a phone call from the legendary "fixer" [and lawyer to both Joe Glaser and Al Capone!] Sidney Korshak. He simply said, "Your loan is forgiven," and hung up.)

Recently, one of my parents' friends talked to me about that house. The friend said that if ever the place came up for sale, they would love to jump in and buy it. This was very moving to me, but I also wondered aloud whether my mother's having been shot there would affect the friend's feelings about the place. The answer was enlightening: "Far from it." My parents' house was a place for Black

Americans—in fact, for all Americans—to engage in positive change. Whether it was athletes or entertainers or politicians or educators or artists, everyone would come and find a haven, a comforting, open arena in which they could express themselves, share what they were doing, move the culture and the country forward. *Everybody* got invited to the Avant house. My parents' friend said, "Why do you think that people like Harry Belafonte, Ted Kennedy, and Andrew Young loved being at your house all the time? They wanted to meet as many people from as many different backgrounds as possible and come up with solutions and positive change. That was so inspiring to me."

And it inspired me, too, because my childhood home had become a beacon of light, a nexus where things got changed—and I got to witness that change firsthand.

But none of this could have happened without my parents' having been welcomed to Trousdale Estates.

These men and women—neighbors, family friends, colleagues—were incredible role models for me, and they gave me a roadmap for my life and what I wanted to do and who I wanted to be.

I, too, get a high from seeing things work out for people, making things happen that maybe couldn't have happened before. My friend Angella, whom I met when she was ten, was regaling us all recently with stories about our child-hoods. She and a few of her friends had come to Beverly Hills from Iran after the revolution. In the Beverly Hills school system, they discovered that they weren't particu-larly welcomed or wanted—they didn't look like us and they spoke a strange language. But I was happy to hear that in the Persian community today, I am remembered as "inclusive."

I didn't have any choice! I remember my dad, after pick-ing me up from school one afternoon, asking me about my day. "There are all these new kids," I said, referring to the Iranian émigrés, "and I feel so bad for them because peo-ple were throwing spitballs at them and teasing them and laughing at them and telling them to go back home."

My father pulled the car over and stopped. "Nicole," he said, "I better not find out that you were one of those kids who made them feel bad. You know our rule: You don't get to wake up and hurt people on purpose. Ever." Point made.

As we drove on, he told me about how Black people had had to integrate schools, how they were beaten up, spit on, and traumatized—daily. For my dad in 1970s Beverly Hills, it was the same shit, even if the targets weren't Black. And he wasn't having it.

The next day, after my father's fierce speech to me, I became friends with Nicky and Monica and Angella and Alona. We're still friends. And I didn't need to be told twice.

✦ ✦ ✦

The challenge for me, surrounded in my growing-up years by extraordinary people, was, Who did *I* want to be? Each of my mentors had integrity, flexibility, and discipline—things that I admire above all else. I learned early that pessimists and people without hope can't create a future. But what did I want to do with the blessings of my ancestors and the beneficence of people like Quincy? Well, I had one advantage that had nothing to do with money or place or anything like that: I could look around me and see men and women who had persevered, had been ready, had fought with dignity for their rights and their freedom. This was the first part of my plan for my life: I had to take their examples and *be* someone—someone who took her history seriously, who listened when these people spoke, and who had something interesting to say when they asked.

This is a question for all of us to be asking ourselves: Who are the positive examples in our lives? Perhaps even more important: What kind of positive example do we share with those around us? What kind of ancestors are we to those we interact with? We don't have to be eighty years old to be an ancestor, or at least to bring the wisdom of an ancestor. When we're faced with a challenge, let's not imagine that we need to have all—or indeed *any*—of the answers. Let's simply wonder, How do we continue the legacy of those whose struggles have given us the advantages we have today? If anyone ever asks me, "What should I do?" I always say, "Do the next right thing, whether someone is looking or not." That's the essence of bearing witness, and of honoring those who raised you.

When you're on someone's shoulders, you can be either a deadweight or a lookout. Why choose the former when you can choose the latter?

❖ ❖ ❖

Clarence Avant was the eldest of eight children. He was raised in Jim Crow's North Carolina, in the no-horse, two-room schoolhouse town of Climax. His was a very poor and tough upbringing, as I've mentioned; he barely knew his birth father, and his stepfather was so abusive that Clarence once put poison in the older man's food. His stepfather didn't eat the food, thank God, but Clarence was clearly no longer safe at home. Before he'd finished ninth grade, he was kicked out of the house and fled to New Jersey to live with his Aunt Annie.

So much for his painful childhood. It has become accepted, I think, that such an upbringing might serve as an explanation, and even a justification, for poor behavior later in life. I don't see it that way. People are good in their hearts, or they're not. We all know of people who've had terrible childhoods and gone on to be loving, successful, kind adults; and we all know of people who've had similarly tough upbringings and have brought havoc to the world.

Some months back, while I was driving on Beverly Boulevard in Los Angeles, I stopped at a light at the intersection with Fairfax. To my right was the Shell station opposite the CBS lot; to my left, the old movie theater, Fairfax Cinemas, where I used to watch *The Sound of Music*. (It's still one of my favorite movies, even though—because?—my mother made me watch it literally hundreds of times.) I thought it was wonderful that so many children were able to see the good and also be aware of bad people who wanted to do bad things.

> When you're on someone's shoulders, you can be either a deadweight or a lookout. Why choose the former when you can choose the latter?

Decades later, as I idled at the intersection humming "The Lonely Goatherd" and "Do-Re-Mi," suddenly I heard somebody screaming. I could tell it was a woman, but I couldn't figure out where the sound was coming from. Scanning the area, I noticed an alleyway, and in it a woman being harassed by some guy. She was shouting, "Please, please . . ." Every time she tried to move past the guy, he'd move the same way she went, as kids do in a playground, but this was violent, intimidating—he was clearly scaring her, threatening her. From a distance it looked as if he had something in his hand, too. A bat? A long knife? The woman was elderly, probably at least sixty-five years old, with a scarf over her head, and she was carrying a couple of grocery bags. As I watched this play out, I couldn't work out why she didn't just turn and run—but then I realized that she was probably afraid he'd attack her if she turned her back.

It was time to get involved. I started honking my horn. The other drivers at the light, apparently unaware of the alley action, looked at me as though I were crazy.

"There's a woman being harassed!" I shouted, rolling my window down. All the while, the good folks of Los Angeles just kept on walking by.

As I sat on the horn, the guy in the alley turned toward me. "Do you want to do something about it?" he taunted. "What are you gonna do? Are you gonna come get me?"

That's all it took. Cursing fit to bust, I got into the left lane, turned, and zoomed into the alley. I wasn't sure if I was going to use my car to scare the man off or actually run him over . . . but something had to save that woman. All my honking and revving of the engine distracted the guy, and the woman made her escape; now it was just me and the lowlife, both angry. I was stopped a few yards from him, my blood pumping hard. Clearly, I hadn't thought this through.

My inner lion took over. "I'm not playing around," I shouted through the open window. "I. Am. Not. Messing. Around." This seemed to give him pause, long enough at least to give me the finger. Then he walked off into the Goodwill half a block along Beverly Boulevard. I drove around the block and parked, then headed into the Goodwill to warn them—and there he was, screaming inside the store.

I figured my involvement should end after I'd alerted the Goodwill staff to what I'd seen. Back in the car, I called Ted to reground myself.

"I hope I never run for political office, because I'm sure all of that is on camera somewhere, and it won't look so good," I said. But the deeper point, beyond the honking and the cursing and the crazy driving, was that no one had thought to get involved; the man's clear mental health issues had apparently convinced people that he shouldn't be held to account.

Blaming everything on mental health problems or homelessness or a combination of the two means that we are all too quick to resign our responsibility to look out for each other. In addition, it becomes shorthand for the acceptance of dangerous behavior.

It felt at that moment that everyone was more concerned about the man being homeless than the woman being innocent. When I told people the story, some said, "But he was homeless . . ."

I said, "Who cares? What I saw was a man threatening a woman, period. I don't care if he lives in a million-dollar house or under a bridge—it doesn't matter. Because he's homeless, should he be allowed to behave just as he pleases, with no consequences?"

What I witnessed was a woman who needed help, and no one showed up for her. That really pissed me off. Perhaps worse than the free pass given to the attacker was the obliviousness of everyone passing by on the sidewalk. They were all, as Peter did, denying Jesus three times. "If I deny I saw anything, then it didn't happen," they seemed to say. But the worst thing anyone can say is "Someone else will do it," or "It's someone else's problem." It's not a long trek from that attitude to turning a blind eye to all instances of injustice, until we all become "willing executioners." I was proud then, reinvigorated by my attempt to help. I've always respected the underdog, which is why I defended kids who were getting bullied in school, like those Iranian girls years earlier. Just as my dad had driven home that message, my mother had also taught me to be empathetic to people who aren't seen, and that day, the woman in the alley was as if invisible to everyone passing by.

In the end, my feelings about the incident on Beverly Boulevard were contained in what I said to Ted as I drove away: "You know what? I don't feel bad about anything I did, because I would have wanted somebody to intervene for me." And I would do it again.

A section from Jesus's Sermon on the Mount, found in Matthew 7:16–20, comes to mind:

You will know them by their fruits. Do men gather grapes from thornbushes or figs from thistles? Even so, every good tree bears good fruit, but a bad tree bears bad fruit. A good tree cannot bear bad fruit, nor can a bad tree bear good fruit. Every tree that does not bear good fruit is cut down and thrown into the fire. Therefore by their fruits you will know them.

Though Jesus was specifically referring to false prophets in this passage, many of us (me included!) take it more widely to mean that all you need to know about someone is what they show you of themselves. Don't listen to what they say; watch what they do. Many people with mental illness live productive, loving lives; it does them a disservice to pin atrocities on mental suffering. My feeling is, look at someone's heart, watch what they do and how they behave, what they stand for, who they show themselves to be. Have compassion; create safe places in which people can be helped and treated; but don't assume that everyone who does something wicked is mentally ill and therefore should not be held accountable. And if someone with a serious mental illness commits a dangerous crime, let's do the compassionate thing for all of us and get that person out of harm's way.

+ + +

None of this is to say that we shouldn't fight injustice—quite the opposite. If a police officer betrays the trust of the public, there should be severe sanctions; if someone is wrongly convicted, there should be a mechanism by which justice is quickly served. And if there is a great injustice perpetrated upon the least of us, we must retain our fire to make it right. We need to bring a fervent spirit to all such issues. The worst thing we can do is simply *accept* that this is the way the world is, without doing anything about it. One of my father's sayings—"It is what it is; what are you going to do about it?"—is crucial for its second half as much as its first.

One day, my father showed almost too much of his spirit, however, and it nearly cost him everything. That story began for him in the law directory office of Martindale-Hubbell in Summit, New Jersey; for the rest of the world, it began in Mississippi.

It was 1955, and my father was twenty-four years old. His job at Martindale-Hubbell was to move heavy legal tomes around the office. One of a few young Black men in that company so tasked, he was considered a solid young worker, reliable and calm, until the day the not-guilty verdicts were passed at the end of the trial of the accused murderers of Emmett Till.

Till, a fourteen-year-old Chicagoan, had been summering in the Mississippi Delta with relatives. One day, a white woman claimed Till had flirted with her in her store, and a few days later, the woman's husband and his half brother abducted Till from Till's great-uncle's house and beat, disfigured, and murdered him. The subsequent trial was a sham and ended in the acquittal of the two men accused of the murder.

When the announcement came down that day in September 1955, Clarence stormed around the Martindale-Hubbell office cursing the injustice, cursing white America, railing on the agony and horror of yet another miscarriage of justice. The president of the company, one Edward Nofer, heard the commotion—it would have been impossible to miss—and pulled Clarence aside. Upon asking the younger man to explain his outburst, Nofer was sympathetic; and he didn't fire my dad, as everyone assumed he would.

Perhaps the reason Nofer was kinder than he might have

been was down to the bravery of Till's mother, Mamie Till Bradley. Nofer, like many Americans, had seen various heart-shattering photographs in the newspapers. Mamie had insisted on an open casket, and photographs of Till's mutilated face were among those that had been widely disseminated, creating an impact in America similar to that of the photograph of a young man named Gordon, also known as "Whipped Peter," during the Civil War. (The photo of Whipped Peter remains heartbreaking and startling, his back covered in thick keloid scars from the abuse he'd received at the hands of slave owners.)

When we *see* such things, our minds are stirred so much more powerfully than when we're just *told* about them. (I, like many people, think it would take only one such explicit photograph from the scene of a school shooting to change the gun laws in the United States, though I could never urge any parent to release such an image to the world. I still marvel at Mamie Till Bradley's extraordinary bravery.) In the case of Mr. Nofer in New Jersey in 1955, it wasn't impossible for him to have imagined that Emmett Till's face could have been my father's face, or the face of any of his other young Black employees. A moral imagination is all it takes, and Mr. Nofer had just such an imagination. To this day my father credits Mr. Nofer with saving his life. "If Nofer would've fired me," my dad said recently, "I would probably have ended up in a terrible place. I had no formal education. I had nothing."

A little while later, Dad started working for Joe Glaser's talent management company. Later still, he would become an eminent manager of talent himself, and a man whom everyone turned to for help and advice. And, when called upon, he also got involved in politics, because he wanted Black Americans to have an effective say in their own lives.

Clarence became a very prominent supporter of many politicians, including Ted Kennedy, Jimmy Carter, Andrew Young, and Bill and Hillary Clinton.

But just as my father had put aside all concerns for his own future by his actions that day in Mr. Nofer's office, so I, too, understood early that "if you're not standing for something, you'll fall for anything," which I took to mean, raise your voice when you see injustice.

Accordingly, there were no sidelines in my house. There was too much painful history to stand by and just watch. We were expected to speak up.

I grew up in a house that had a revolving door of famous people coming to parties, to meetings, to see my father and mother, so I had plenty of opportunity to speak. So many people came to our living room: Ella Fitzgerald, Josephine

Baker, Maya Angelou, Diahann Carroll, Cicely Tyson, James Baldwin, Harry Belafonte, the King family—Coretta Scott King wrote my parents to thank them for their "marvelous contribution to the continuation of my husband's work"—and the author of *Roots*, Alex Haley, who similarly wrote "in admiration of the symbol for us which I feel that you represent." Muhammad Ali came by regularly: I recall him saying once, "The service we give others is the rent we pay for our room in the hereafter." I found myself using his words to reframe my way of thinking until I realized that through my energy I could be a blessing and a sermon and of service *wherever* I find myself.

Baseball legend Hank Aaron was a regular visitor, too; he'd had to face down the full weight of a racist country when he was setting all those batting records for the Braves and Brewers and when he eventually broke Babe Ruth's home-run record. But it was what came after breaking the record that my father cared about. Black people needed endorsement deals, too, and my father made it his business to live by the mantra "If it's good enough for white people, it's good enough for Black people." My father eventually got Aaron an endorsement deal with Coca-Cola as the home-run record approached. (Legendarily, my father walked into the office of the president of Coca-Cola and simply said, "N-----s drink Coke too.") My father also got deals for Jim Brown and Ali, and I got to witness all of those developments.

The people in my living room understood that they held the power to reinvent themselves. They took the challenge of renewing their minds every day, which allowed them to overcome their circumstances. My mom understood that putting me in the room with these positive influences would lead to powerful thoughts that would then lead to positive feelings that would then turn into better decisions, which would decide my actions, behavior, and character—she understood that my character would play a huge role in my destiny. And I figured out at a very young age that it's impossible to change your circumstances without renewing your mind and choosing different thoughts—only then can you create a change on the outside.

From these role models, I learned not to be a silent witness.

One night in the early eighties, the legendary Maxine Waters came by the house. Back then, she was a member of the California State Assembly, but already a titan of California politics. (She would enter the US House of Representatives in 1991, where she remains in her eighties!) As a youngster, I used to skateboard on the Venice Beach boardwalk as often as I was allowed. Unfortunately, it was becoming a very dangerous place to hang out—open drug use was rife, and it wasn't unusual to see fights on the boardwalk, all of which terrified me.

So that night, during a dinner party my parents hosted, I took Maxine to task for how dangerous Venice had become, asking her what she, as the state assemblywoman for the 48th District, planned to do about it.

I was eleven years old.

My mother loved that moment; encouraged it; reminded me of it even when I was old enough to roll my eyes at the memory of the audacity of a kid in middle school pushing her opinions on an experienced politician. But the point is, there was no "kids' table" in my house; we were expected to have opinions, to speak up—to listen, yes, but then to step forward, as my father had done in 1955 and so many times since.

We were expected to *be* someone.

Of course, just because politics was everywhere, it didn't mean that we necessarily always picked the winning side!

◆ ◆ ◆

As I mentioned, my father used his hard-fought connections in the entertainment world to open the door to political candidates, too, people who, much like himself, had often heard the word *no*.

Dad raised money for underdogs, like a peanut farmer from Georgia with the surname Carter, and a smooth-talking governor from Arkansas, last name Clinton. I remember, when I was in college, calling my parents one day and being shocked to find out that they were flying to Arkansas for dinner. In my political ignorance, I said, "Who on earth do you know in Arkansas, and why would you be going to visit?"

My dad said, "This guy, Bill Clinton, is going to be the president of the United States."

"No way, Dad," I said, with the confidence that could come only from being a communications major at California State University, Northridge—"No way a guy from Arkansas is going to be the president of the United States! Nu-uh."

Dad went anyway, of course.

Years later, Dad said to me, "There's a guy I'm going to go see in Chicago. He's a state senator; people think he's a big deal. He wants to meet me." Then Dad laughed and said, "I don't know where he thinks he's going with that crazy name of his."

After their meeting, my dad reported that he'd really liked the guy with the supposedly crazy name (but he also *never* said, "I think this guy's going to be president," as he had about Bill Clinton). He remained loyal to the Clinton family via his support of Hillary, which I respected.

Cut to the early 2000s, and this man with the unusual

name—Barack Hussein Obama, of course—came to Los Angeles to do some fundraising for his US Senate race. When we met, I liked his vibe, his ease, his calm; and his name was perfectly *fine*, of course. I wanted a candidate to better represent the kind of Americans you see out on the street in every town, so I got involved because there was no way I could *not*.

+ + +

I find myself coming back to energy yet again. Policy is important, of course; politics is important as well; but *energy* is what drives my enthusiasm. Barack's energy is the first, the middle, and the last thing you notice about him. You can disagree with his politics all you like, but compare his energy to what came after and you'll see what I mean.

Your energy follows your thoughts—in fact, energy follows *everything*. When we speak positively, energy follows. Negatively? It follows that too. That's why keeping positive energy can only help to create a better, more positive life.

I followed this mantra closely after what happened to my mother.

Almost instantly, I was faced with a question of what energy to bring to these terrifying moments. I'd been woken from sleep by the most devastating phone call imaginable—

"Nicole, your mom's been shot"—and instantly I had to marshal either a negative energy or a positive one.

It would have been natural, I think, to have lain frozen in my bed, unable to move due to the horror I'd been faced with, and yet my mother's example filled and drove me. She had never fallen into negativity, even when the worst that could possibly happen had happened. In the mid-1970s, Clarence had faced terrible financial straits: he was losing his radio station, KAGB (one of the only Black-owned stations on the West Coast), and his record label, Sussex, was folding; in addition, he'd been unable to pay Bill Withers, and Bill had understandably "moved on," as he put it. With everything happening at once, we **Choose kindness. Choose life.** also faced losing the beloved house, as I mentioned earlier.

When asked about it years later, this is what my mother said about those years: "You don't leave. You're in this together, so you wait it out, but you have to *face* it. You can't make believe it didn't happen."

So that morning of my mother's death, I felt that same force in me. I was in this with her, we were together; and I had to face whatever it was that awaited me. *You can't make believe it didn't happen.*

But the first thing that needed to be done was to feed the dogs. They were defenseless without me; I had no idea how long I'd be gone, and none of this could be explained to a pair of beautiful animals. So that's what I did—in the face of whatever was coming, I chose life, something positive, a simple moment of care that set the tone for everything that came after.

Feed the dogs. Let them out. Choose kindness. Choose life.

+ + +

On Barack's subsequent visits to Los Angeles I would introduce him to people, and once he became a US senator, we put together a coalition of folks who would keep supporting him. All of us were getting involved because, as I said above, there was no way we could not. It helped that, in my case, that's what I'd seen my parents do.

My mother was someone who'd always gotten involved in important issues: in the 1970s, she was the president of an organization called Neighbors of Watts, a support group for the South Central Community Child Care Center, which was created after the riots in August 1965—she raised money, bought books, and supported the arts and music in a troubled part of town. Going forward, her name will be attached to the new Jacqueline Avant Children and Family Center on the MLK Medical Campus, also in Watts.

The list of her involvements was remarkably long. She served on the board of directors of the International Student Center at UCLA, on the board of the Wallis Annenberg Center for the Performing Arts, and as board president of the Museum of African American Art in Los Angeles. Her love of Japanese art (*love* is too weak a word—she in fact had one of the biggest collections of Japanese lacquer *in the country*) led her to signing up as a docent in the Pavilion for Japanese Art at the Los Angeles County Museum of Art. That love was sparked after she read an eleventh-century Japanese novel, *The Tale of Genji*, when she was in college.

Her spectacular Japanese collection was celebrated at the Crow Museum of Asian Art in Dallas in 2013, and I'd say that this was one of her proudest moments. But for her, Japanese lacquer was not simply something to collect—she had a personal, spiritual connection to each piece of art she selected.

Much as she loved art, Mom was more likely to spend money on practical items. A few weeks before she died, she bought more than three hundred bikes for kids in Watts, *just because.* "Sweet Alice" Harris, her friend and a community activist, told a reporter for ABC-7, "[Jacqueline Avant] said, 'Don't tell anybody else.' She is the only one who ever said, 'I'm going buy all the bikes you'll ever need.'"

All the bikes you'll ever need—that's all anyone ever needed to know about Jacqueline Avant. That said it all.

+ + +

The details of Barack Obama's upbringing are well known to many of us. His father was from Kenya, his mother was from Kansas; he was born in Honolulu, where his parents were studying. After his parents divorced (when Barack was tiny), the boy was mostly raised by his mother, and when he was six, his mother and her new husband moved the family to Indonesia. Returning to Honolulu at age ten, Barack moved in with his grandparents.

Obama has talked about how hard it was to know who he was, so varied was his background, so challenging his childhood. From such an uncomfortable start in life, how could he have dreamed of a presidency? A lot of people prayed and toiled for Obama, as they did for me, because they knew something was coming. They may never have seen it themselves, but they knew it was coming.

Each time Barack came to town as a state senator, I brought people to meet him, as I noted earlier. Once he became a US senator, pretty soon somebody said that he was going to run for president. I said, "That's completely insane. He just got to Washington. He needs to wait a minute; he needs to serve in the US Senate for a while."

Eventually I headed to Washington to meet with Obama's presidential campaign, but I still felt it was too early for

Barack, and I wasn't open to the promptings of what was in the air. It's easy to look back in hindsight and wonder how I could not jump at the chance; hindsight is always so convincing. But the problem was, I was looking at the issue from the wrong end of the telescope. I still couldn't see what others saw in me, which, though it looks like modesty, can also be a front for ego.

Fortunately, I knew some of my strengths, too. I'm a good communicator; I love bringing people together and making great connections. I love to serve and problem-solve. The truth is, I simply love to help. So, when I was told that my friend Charlie Rivkin was going to be involved in Barack's campaign, that was the clincher for me. I'm embarrassed to say that my committing to that job was initially more about working with Charlie than working with Barack!

One of the first places I turned was my own backyard. Every political event I'd ever been to basically consisted of white people talking to white people about what white people needed (and even white people talking to Black people about what Black people needed, which was all the more frustrating!). What was missing were the committed Latina women, the powerful Black women, the accomplished Asian women—women of all colors and creeds, all of whom have influence and power and smarts and money. When it came to the movement for Obama, it couldn't look like every other presidential campaign because *he* didn't look like every other presidential candidate. Both he and the campaign had to mirror what America looks like.

So I started having meetings around LA. I wanted to do things differently. At a meeting with my co-chairs, I stuck my neck out. "I've grown up in this world [of LA privilege] and here's the problem," I said. "Every time we have political events, they're always in Brentwood or the Palisades. And they're all white. But there are Latina women, there are Black women, there are Asian women, there are Persian women in Los Angeles who have influence, who have power, who have smarts, and who have money. And I'm going to be the one to introduce you to all of them."

And that's what I did—I started calling everybody.

"Do you know a really powerful Latina woman I could call right now?" I asked one friend.

"Giselle Fernandez!" my friend said. "She's amazing."

I called her. "Can you bring together a coalition of people of color in the LA area for Barack?" I asked Giselle. And she did.

Then I called my friends in Beverly Hills, Brentwood, View Park, and Baldwin Hills. All the women I'd called, along with those Giselle had called, met in the backyard of Giselle's house. There was a different feeling to this campaign; as hoped, it felt much more like a mirror of our diverse

America than usual. In large part because of that diverse representation, when Michelle Obama showed up at her first luncheon in Los Angeles, we raised over $100,000!

No one questioned anything in the campaign after that.

But it wasn't just fundraising. What I'd learned from my parents is that you have to bring everybody into a room and let them get to know each other if you want to bring about change; everything is about *connection*.

The importance of personal connection is one of the reasons the pandemic was so damaging; even despite Zoom, our physical distancing stopped people looking each other directly in the eye and truly connecting. I'm sure eye contact is what so many of my ancestors counted on; they didn't allow their poor background or lack of opportunity to be a barrier to real connection. My father still has a firm handshake, even in his nineties; and he looks at people, directly in the eye, assessing them. My mother was the same. She showed up; she knew that being in the room was just as important as—more important than!—merely raising money from a distance.

In those early meetings I put together for Barack, there were eminent doctors, lawyers, real estate agents, business owners, all of them just as successful as the next one—and none of them knew each other. I needed to start building little coalitions; creating nodes from which connections could be made. Never underestimate the power of networks.

Lots of people are allergic to networking, but that's because it's seen as entirely transactional.

It shouldn't be. Networking is most effective when people learn from each other, rather than trying to get something out of every interaction. Again, leaving the ego at the door is the key to making progress in life. If you shut up and listen, as my father did in those early meetings, you'll be amazed at what you hear, what you learn.

At one meeting at the Buffalo Club in Santa Monica, I told folks I needed them to be my army.

"Go find as many two-hundred-dollar people as possible," I said. One friend found thirty people, and then someone else did the same, and someone else . . .

What we were building wasn't just a fund; it was what I'd seen my father do all those years: we were building a community. We were raising ourselves up. We weren't waiting for anyone to give us a green light or permission to make a difference. We had seen a need—a need, in this case, for a new kind of politics in which everyone got a seat at the table—and we had stepped up to make it happen.

For women, but especially for women of color, sometimes the culture views us as invisible. As Charlie would say, "I thought I knew about sexism, but I didn't fully understand it until I saw it firsthand with Nicole." I would put together these events for the Obamas, but when I'd walk into the room with Charlie, people wouldn't even look at me—instead, they'd just congratulate Charlie.

Charlie would say, "This is *Nicole's* event. I had nothing to do with it." (It was, after all, often a woman's event!)

By the end of the fundraising drive for Barack Obama, there were probably a thousand people at any one time in the Los Angeles area looking at their phones and thinking, "Oh no, it's Nicole Avant. What now? What are we fixing today?" but no one from the campaign second-guessed me anymore.

I guess in a way I've assumed something like my father's role when it comes to moving people forward: I just want to introduce everyone to everyone and let them work out how to best make the world better. Clarence was always in the background, too, but he brought people together and made magic happen.

I was thirty-nine, a political baby. People had just assumed I was merely going through my dad's Rolodex, when in fact I'd also learned from his way of putting people together. More important, I'd learned from, and was leaning heavily on, the lessons of my mother—a woman who could run rings around most people.

How do you think I know how to do all this stuff anyway?

THE UNOPENED CHRISTMAS CARD

When something terrible happens somewhere, it's natural enough, I suppose, to imagine that the place where it happened is tainted, haunted, spoiled, ruined forever. I completely understand why the school at Sandy Hook was razed and why plans are in place to do the same to Robb Elementary School in Uvalde, Texas. Amazingly, there's a government program to fund such demolitions. This is the world in which we live.

But there's something about my parents' house that defies what happened there; the place has an aura, a spirit, that couldn't be extinguished by two minutes of violence. It's not a mess. There's no bad energy there.

My mom didn't die in the house, thank God. (One of the officers told me that he's seen similar injuries to twenty-year-old gang members, and they were gone in an instant; my mother hung on until she made it to the hospital.)

If you didn't know about what befell her there, what you'd notice when you entered that property is hummingbirds whizzing back and forth, the sound of the wind blowing through the trees. That place has the most beautiful energy.

The Unopened Christmas Card

But still, right after the incident, we didn't know what we'd find there. And someone needed to go to my parents' house and get things for my dad.

In the days after it happened, I was fortunate to be loved by a group of people who weren't wailing and carrying on. They didn't need me to lift them up, as can sometimes happen when people are faced with a tragedy; they just knew what to do. They each knew what their gifts were and put themselves to work. This team sat around in my kitchen, divvying up the tasks. No questions—just action.

I didn't need to think about food or how I was going to host and feed the large number of people who were showing up at my house daily—but my dear friend Irena did. Irena, who is gorgeous on the inside and outside, put together a system that fed us all for at least six weeks— we had more cheese plates, Chinese food, Italian food, soul food, you name it, than we could ever finish. And each offering showed up with love and without any effort on our part. Irena was grace in action. *All* of my friends were. Not to mention my father's very close friends Irving and Shelli. Theirs had been one of the first calls I'd received after we lost my mom, and from that moment on, Nate and Al's deli food arrived daily. (I'm still working it off!)

It was Amy and Danielle, my friend, and my roommate from college, who went to my parents' place after the detectives had finished their work (but before it was cleaned up) to get my father's things and whatever else they thought we'd want.

Amy said, "I need to go in there, and I'm good at this. I know it was recently a crime scene. But I'm not afraid of blood. I'm not scared of anything."

Amy went back to my parents' house three more times; and yes, she saw the bullet holes, but she kept on going. She opened all the windows, burned sage, said every Jewish prayer she knew. (By the way—she was two months pregnant when she did all this. I'm now the proud godmother to her daughter, Lincoln Alexandra.)

Once she had assessed her task, Amy went to the Container Store and bought thirty containers and bubble wrap. She then grabbed whatever she thought was necessary from the house. "I felt like your mom was telling me what you would like," Amy explained. "So I went to every room and grabbed whatever she said I had to get." Amy wrapped that stuff to the point where I still can't even open the packages; she wrapped them tight with love.

One day, Amy found the Christmas card that my mom

had chosen for me. It was brand new, not yet written on. Sitting on her desk. Still in the plastic.

The things we lose when we lose someone are the smallest things, and the biggest: an unopened Christmas card, still in the plastic. But we gain a great deal, too. Amy's brave soul, stronger, tougher, more loving now than ever, shone for all of us then. And a home, where so much of American life had passed through, a home that was always open to everyone, was still that: just the home I grew up in, filled with the energy of lives well lived. That home is not a place of horror, or sorrow, or agony, or destruction.

It's where my mother lived. It's where my mother lives.

FOUR

Service Industry

Not so many years ago when I was home for a visit (I've lived in NYC for many years), I ran into your mom on Robertson with my mom. I felt as if it was my lucky day. Although it had been years, it was as if nothing had changed. She was warm, gracious, and genuinely interested in hearing about my life. I know she made everyone feel so special.

These days, my father gets up every morning and reads the *New York Times* cover to cover. He's ninety-one now, but he's still engaged, still interested, still determined to be fully informed, and still extremely opinionated. (These opinions are often punctuated with more swear words than any sentence should be able to bear. In fact, some statements he utters are made up entirely of imprecations—no nouns, verbs, adjectives, prepositions, pronouns, adverbs, or conjunctions—just expletives, separated by a powerful look from piercing eyes.)

Every day, at the end of his reading of the newspaper, he heads to the obituaries section to, I quote, "check I'm not motherfuckin' there."

My father, even though he's lost his lifelong companion, is still living . . . but what does it mean to live after a loss like this? How are we to continue after such a bereavement, after the driving force of our family has been torn from us by a random act of violence? For my father, I think it has something to do with the rhythm of his life—he's always bounced from triumph to tragedy, tragedy to triumph. As he says himself, "I always found a place to lay my head." As a young child, his family was so dirt poor that his mother used to boil a sweet potato, pulled out of the very earth, so he'd have something to take with him to eat at school. (That's how he got his nickname, Sweet Potato.) And he still remembers the name of the girl on the school bus who, instead of teasing him as others did, shared her sandwich with him: Helen Goen.

Recently, I watched a documentary about how the people of Aberfan reacted after their terrible tragedy in 1966. The little Welsh mining town was devastated by a destructive flow of debris from one of the mines—tons of debris that rushed down a mountainside during heavy rains into the village, where it buried the local grade school. In all, 116 children and 28 adults died that terrible October day. Something that one of the grieving mothers said in the documentary struck me: "The village went quiet; everything went quiet. I don't think anybody left their homes for a long, long time; a lot of people didn't leave their homes for years."

Such a reaction is entirely understandable in the face of unspeakable tragedy. The overwhelming nature of loss can take away energy, agency, drive, joy—so much so that people in Aberfan simply holed up in their houses, paralyzed by their pain.

I get it; I truly do. We're taught from an early age that death is a visitation from the beyond, something we'll never understand, something that it's almost obscene to "get over." In our closure-obsessed world, the one thing we give ourselves a pass for is not finding closure after a bereavement.

But if there's one thing upon which we can rely, in a world where everything is in flux, death is the surest constant. It will happen to all of us. Our job is to decide how to face it; how to live after the death of a loved one; and how to live our own lives with the sure knowledge that one day we, too, will secure a final date for our obituary notice.

It's difficult, sometimes, to fight against people's expectations of what grief is supposed to look like. I knew, after my mother's death, that I was supposed to be in the fetal position, wailing and gnashing my teeth (and there were times that happened, for sure—don't get me wrong). That was all anyone was expecting of me then, and because I wasn't doing those things, I could sense questions: "Why are you not devastated?" "Why are you able to get up and do things?" I would always have to explain, "I *am* grieving; I'm just moving through it."

I give my mom full credit for this strength. She gave me the tools to build the ark for when the floods arrived. She forced me to buckle up when the storms came. She didn't allow me to fold and hide until things were safe again. I had to face whatever was coming my way—death, sickness, disappointment, betrayal. Her lessons made me constantly ask myself what kind of person I wanted to become when faced with hard times—because there *will be* hard times, for all of us. In one way or another, the trials inevitably show up and the storms always blow, and I choose to be a person who faces them whether I'm ready or not.

In the last few months, I have decided to keep moving forward, living life, because guess what? The sun is still rising. The moon is coming out. As Jesus tells us in Matthew 6:26–29:

Look at the birds of the air, for they neither sow nor reap nor gather into barns; yet your heavenly Father feeds them. Are you not of more value than they? Which of you by worrying can add one cubit to his stature? So why do you worry about clothing? Consider the lilies of the field, how they grow: they neither toil nor spin; and yet I say to you that even Solomon in all his glory was not arrayed like one of these.

The point is that the world goes on, whatever happens within it. So I knew life wasn't going to stop for me.

But I don't want anyone to imagine that it's been easy. Most nights, I lie in my bathtub and talk to Mom. Our final text exchange had been as I'd been preparing to take a bath, so naturally each night my mind turns toward her as the steaming water rises. There's still so much to say that I didn't get a chance to say; still so many things I'd like to ask my mom that I never got to ask. What, am I supposed to just bury those questions with her? Am I supposed to watch the water swirl down the drain and let my connection with her seep away too? It's not enough that the world visited upon my family this horror—are we to consign ourselves to silence? So I talk to my mother every night as I take my bath. I couldn't tell you what I say. And in fact it doesn't matter; it's just connection, memory transmuted into the present, a kind of divination—a grief-stricken daughter talking to her lost mother, hoping to find a roadmap for the future. It's not a question, either, of whether Mom talks back; the mere act of conversation, one way or another, is enough.

One thing I'm sure of—she wants me busy, wants me moving forward. After all, I have things to do. When the disaster happened, there were two movies I was producing; there were two public boards I was about to join.

Then there was Universal.

I had been nominated to the board of Universal Music Group, and I was faced with a choice when I was invited to visit the offices on April 19, 2022—the same day that the person who shot and killed my mother was being sentenced. Should I decline and stay home, keeping my grief quietly behind the walls of my house, or should I step out into the world?

My parents had prepared me for this. I give credit to them for my ability to move forward, regardless of what I'm facing. They didn't realize, of course, that they were preparing me for that specific day, but they did; and in that moment, I decided that I wasn't going to give away any more time or power to that murderer—I was going to stay in the present moment and show up for myself.

The storms always blow, and I choose to be a person who faces them whether I'm ready or not.

My mom got killed, yes, but I was determined to use what I'd learned from her when faced with my own Calvary. Luke 22:42 says it well: "Father, if it is Your will, take this cup away from Me; nevertheless not My will, but Yours, be done." I had to learn how to not retreat but take what had been given to me and move forward.

So I duly showed up to meet some of the team. As I walked through the Universal building, I could feel eyes upon me—"Oh my God, that's the daughter. Why is *she* here?"

I was determined, though: I was not giving that man who'd killed my mother anything.

Ted, that morning, had said, "You could call them and postpone—they'd understand."

"I don't care if they understand," I told him. "What else am I going to do? Sit here and cry all day?"

So off I went to Santa Monica for my meeting. When I walked into the meeting room, I found my friend Sherry already there.

"Oh my God," Sherry said, looking up from her phone, "what are you doing here?"

"I wasn't about to give this meeting over to him," I said.

"Look at you, all made up!" she said, noticing that I was very put together that day. I presume she'd imagined that if I turned up, I'd be a mess. Well, I did indeed turn up, and I wasn't a mess. I *was* put together—I had my face on!

"Nothing is guaranteed," I said, "and God forbid I go tomorrow. You think I'm going to give that fucker anything else?"

And yes, I said *fucker*—I'm not my father's daughter for nothing. "It's life, Sherry," I said. "I have to move with it. It flows like water. Yes, there will be blips in it, even tsunamis. But everything else was functioning today, so why shouldn't I? The birds still woke up to sing today. The traffic roared by. Everything keeps going. This is what my mother would want me to be: undaunted."

But I wasn't *trying* to be strong. I wasn't trying to be anything. I was just trying to live. The greatest gift I could give my mother was to live. I've traveled all around the world and seen innumerable people who literally don't have a pot to piss in . . . but they're living—they choose to *live*, period, amen. Who am I to think I'm an exception? So many people don't have that choice; why should I have it?

I know now that my parents—my mother, especially—truly were preparing me for a terrible day like this. The lesson was this: it's not about the loss and the death—it's about the *life*, the dash between the dates (as my dad would say). That, there, is truly the art of living.

In eighth grade, for a class assignment, we had to write our own obituary. The teacher asked us, "What do you think people would say about you?"

I remember being stumped at that age and going home to talk to my mom about it.

"I don't know *what* people would say, or even what I'd want them to think about me," I said.

My mother just let me talk. In the end, I concluded that I wanted people to think that I was a good person and that I wanted to help others.

No, really, that was all I came up with. "Mom!" I wailed. "It's too short!"

My mother had a very simple but profound answer to my complaint. "The more you do and the more you're out in the world, the more they'll have to write about," she said. "If you're out living a life and you're serving people and making a positive difference in people's lives, and if people smile when your name is mentioned, well, that's what they're going to write about you—how you made people feel seen, loved, supported . . ."

Her point was, you haven't lived yet, but one day, make sure you do. That day at Universal, and in fact all the days since my mother died, I've been out in the world, living a life, serving people, trying to make a difference.

In the weeks after Mom died, I received countless notes from people saying, "Wow, is this your mom? I never knew all the things she was involved in," or, "I'm reading about your mom, and her life was incredible!" I just smiled each time, because I knew already that she'd lived life fully—or, as my father might put it, "she *did* shit." She made sure that she was always involved, but it was never about her.

That's her legacy in me, now. Showing up, being involved, trying to make a positive change. And I'm drawn to those who do the same.

Like me, my mother learned her attitude from others. She had been mentored in her early years by a woman named Harriette Evans Shields, who ran a series of children's centers in Watts. Harriette was like a second mom to my mom. Harriette shone a light on what was happening in Watts, and in turn, my mother shone a light for her friends in Beverly Hills.

The Watts section of LA is less than ten miles as the crow flies from the Trousdale Estates where we lived, but it might as well be on a different planet. Watts has always struggled with poverty and its attendant privations and violence, but my mother wasn't about to let children suffer in her adopted city on what she felt was her watch. (Of course, she felt *everything* was her watch.) But my mother also knew the limitations: "We cannot save everyone," she said, "but there are some people there—children and parents—who are not making bad choices; their struggle is not their fault. They want to go to safe schools, they want to be able to afford books . . ."

She first took me to Watts when I was about ten years old. A young girl had died there in a hit-and-run. We didn't know the girl, but that didn't matter to my mother, and she was sure it shouldn't matter to me, despite my protestations. There was a funeral, and we were going to attend (and help pay both for it and for the food afterward). I watched as my mother prepared plates for people, deep in their grief. All this was to get me out of my young comfort zone. These were people who through no fault of their own had very little, and she needed me to see that.

That's just one of the reasons why she got involved in Watts, and remained so all those years. It was time to step up. I took that as my model, but especially after my mother died. It became the only way I knew how to grieve.

+ + +

My father's survival is based on my mother's strength and leadership, as they flow through me. It's that simple. I'm negotiating grief for myself, yes, but also for Clarence and for my brother, Alex.

Mom served our family directly, too. That terrible night, my dad was asleep in the back part of the house, and the police think my mother surprised the intruder. Because she didn't call out for Clarence, it's not an exaggeration to say that she probably saved my father's life. Her protective shield was extra strong that night.

My mother died, but she lives, too, in so many ways we're only just discovering.

◆ ◆ ◆

For years my mother had been focused on the wellness center at Martin Luther King Medical Center in Watts. My friend Candace had been taking her down there as they worked on where to build a new facility. My mother was adamant about where it should go: "No, I don't like it so close to the freeways," she'd say—or something like it—until they found the perfect spot. After her death the center unanimously voted to rename the new building after her, and we've already raised more than half a million dollars since that fateful December. My mom was always bothered by children being sick and not being able to have their families with them, so that's been the focus of the design and construction—a light, joyful place filled with books and toys and even the odd clown!

All these efforts feel as if my mother was working toward a legacy, and when I think about the time surrounding her death, a nagging sense of her knowing something, expecting something, keeps tugging on my cuff. The day before she died, there had been yet another mass shooting in a school, this time in Oxford, Michigan, and I knew she'd be devastated by it—she always was, especially after Sandy Hook. Whenever there was a mass shooting, she would shut down in complete disbelief. My mother felt everything keenly, like the artist she undoubtedly was. (She dreamed of being a news journalist or an editor; I think part of the reason behind her pushing me so hard was a sense that her full potential had remained just out of reach.)

So there was already a heaviness in those early winter days. My mother had noticed it—she'd called her friend Neil and had said, "I don't feel right. Something's weird. The security lights are out." Neil showed up, but still Mom was perturbed. "I still don't feel quite right." The night of her death I spoke with her, but she was tired—and then she spoke to my cousin Barry and told him how proud she was of him. And he got to tell her that he loved her. Then she and I texted about sweet potato pie, of all things . . .

But perhaps it wasn't an inkling—maybe that's just who she was: someone prepared, every day, that it might be her last. This has become something of a cliché—to live life as if each day were your last, because one day you'll be right. And despite it being a tried-and-tested trope, I still marvel at how many chances we all need to relearn its truth. We don't live forever; we never know the time—so are we, metaphorically at least, buying all the bicycles we can each and every day? How many obituaries do we need to read in the *New York Times*, or how many do we need to write for ourselves in middle school (!), to understand that this is life, right now, every day. It's not *about to start*; we're already *in it*.

I laugh every time I hear the comedian Pete Holmes point out how crazy it is that we Angelenos complain about the traffic . . . because if you're sitting in traffic, you *are* the traffic. That's true of life, too—you *are* life; this is it, it's happening now, and for as long as you draw breath. Blink and it's gone. As Jesus reminds us in the passage quoted above, "Which of you by worrying can add one cubit to his stature?" No amount of thinking or waiting will add to the world's joy or happiness. It's only by *doing* that we honor the legacy of those who can no longer be with us.

◆ ◆ ◆

Can you imagine what my father has been through? It wouldn't have been unreasonable of him to say, "I'm out, I'm done. I'm going to crawl into bed and stay there." He could have died of a broken heart; he could have given up.

But something about my mother's way of living created for him, and for all of us, a roadmap for the future. I see my mother's influence when I hear Dad talk about the man who did this. He's angry, for sure, but he's actually angrier at the guy's parents. That's where my dad's brain went: the parents, the grandparents. "Where the fuck is his family?" That's my dad's question.

I also think that some souls are just stronger than others. My father's soul is made of an extraordinarily dense metal.

But I also believe it's up to all of us to give our most to life. That way, death doesn't have to dominate; if we've lived a full life, and given of ourselves freely and often, then death need not be a moment in which we bemoan all that might have been. We hear in Romans 6:4: "Therefore we were buried with Him through baptism into death, that just as Christ was raised from the dead by the glory of the Father, even so we also should walk in newness of life." This is one of the central lessons of the resurrection: the all-consuming fire of death can, if we choose to let it, give us a freshness in life.

My mother's verve and commitment and involvement in causes have lasted well beyond her death in her legacy, and in how my father strives on, in how I push forward. I have far too much to do to wallow in widow's weeds. I'm navigating this grief for my family, as I just noted, and it's my mother herself—her strength and leadership—who's getting us through these darkest of times. Can I wait to help others later, once the pain eases? Hell no—I'm looking ahead to the next presidential election; I worked in Los Angeles on a mayoral campaign; I'm producing a film on incredible women from the Second World War (the 6888th Central Postal Directory Battalion, also known as the Six Triple Eight). Countless causes that I'm passionate about need my ongoing support. I'm not stopping; all must be done now.

Like my mother, I'm both leading and working out how best I can support leaders. In this effort, I feel deeply connected to my mother, who was one of the driving forces behind my father's successes. But how does one guide one's own destiny and not take a back seat while also supporting? This is what my grief work

I'm not a victim, nor is my family. We're victors.

is channeling: my mother's delicate balancing act of self and selflessness. This is something so many women face: How do we assert ourselves and at the same time bring the great benefits of our natural succor to those around us? My healing, and my navigation of these issues, is in my *doing*. As I've said many times: Put it all on my schedule.

In my grief, I was faced with a challenge, too, which was how to let people in who wanted to help. I think many of my friends expected to be turned away when they showed up, but I knew quickly that my job was to invite people to share the burden. I have one dear friend whose mother has been having some serious health issues, and I've checked in regularly—I'm not going to let anything trigger me, to use the modern phrase. It's all about expansion, not limitation. How else are we to break free of the list of things we've been taught to feel in grief? This is nothing short of a paradigm shift, as I see it. My self-care and my continued efforts to make real change around me are the opposite of a victim story.

I'm not a victim, nor is my family. We're victors.

THE TWELVE POLICE CARS

I forgot to tell you—we have guests tonight." I was on the phone with our security team; I was always forgetting to tell them our plans.

"Yes, ma'am," the agent said kindly. "I'm aware."

"You are?" I said.

"Yes, ma'am," he said. "The Secret Service alerted us."

"Oh, right. I guess that's what the Secret Service does!" I said.

Ted overheard me. "Nicole," he said, "did you not notice the twelve police cars outside?"

Apparently not!

♦ ♦ ♦

A few days earlier, I'd gotten a call.

"We're not going to Hawaii without seeing him," the president had said. Every year, the Obamas spend Christmas in Hawaii, where Barack grew up. But this year, they would be making a detour to see Clarence beforehand.

How I wished they hadn't needed to do so.

Think You'll Be Happy

The evening of their visit, the five of us sat around, chatting. I was looking at my dad, who was talking to the president of the United States. Here as our guest was the man who had a crazy name, the man my father had initially been skeptical of, and the man my father hadn't backed—he'd gone with his old friend Hillary Clinton. But all this was long in the past. Barack had served two terms, and Hillary had become secretary of state; Michelle had become a force in American life, one with just as much to offer as her husband. Now we were sitting in our house, five of us, not six, my mother's death still painfully fresh, while outside, men in dark suits murmured into their cuffs and kept a wary eye on our neighborhood.

What can anyone say? This thought has come to me many times since the loss of my mother, and my answer is always the same. Just say *something*. Just show up. When something this monumental happens in life, there is nothing transformative that can be said—language doesn't work like that. If there were the right words to say, someone would have said them long ago. But there are not the right words; and so often, all of us fall back instead on words that are the opposite of helpful:

"I know how you feel." Nope, no one ever could— what's more, I wouldn't want them to.

"Let me know if there's anything I can do." I don't have the headspace to give you a task; I'm sorry.

"At least . . ." Any sentence spoken to a person grieving that begins with those two words cannot possibly have a good outcome.

So what *is* the answer? What *are* the right words?

Try "I love you." Showing up is everything, as is love.

That night, the Obamas showed up. Michelle gave me the tightest hug and now was holding my hand. Occasionally, Barack turned to talk to Ted about this and that, and when he did so, I sometimes caught my dad gazing off into the distance. The son of poverty and Jim Crow, the young man who'd railed against the horror of Emmett Till, Joe Glaser's mentee, the man who had brought so many people together from so many walks of life, all to his house in Los Angeles, a place no amount of horror could affect . . . a man who had helped Jim Brown and Hank Aaron and Muhammad Ali and so many others—now here that man was, in a gilded room in Hancock Park, chatting with the first Black president and the former first lady.

Clarence was no longer poor. In fact, he was and is rich in a great many things—a man in his nineties who sits out in the garden on sunny days and listens to my Spotify playlist of seventies classics while he does his gentle calisthenics, keeping his blood moving, his mind alert, his handshake sturdy. So many things he still had, there in a room with Barack and Michelle, and still has today—things he could never have imagined back in the town of Climax as a child. But still, despite that richness of wealth and circumstance and opportunity, something fundamental was missing, that night and forever.

FIVE

Finding a New Way
to Grieve

She was such an incredible woman who
always made me feel so welcomed and
loved. I can remember her hug as if it
was yesterday.

When, in August 2021, the Academy Museum of Motion Pictures in Los Angeles named their new grand lobby in honor of Sir Sidney Poitier, who is my honorary godfather, the *Hollywood Reporter* asked me to comment on it. I told them: "I don't think it's coincidental that it's the entry because [Sidney Poitier] represents the entry. He opened doors for so many others."

Sidney had a great many roadblocks facing him from birth. Growing up on Cat Island in the Bahamas, the son of a poor farmer, he never saw a single car, nor did his family own something as basic as a fridge. When Sidney left the Bahamas and headed to Miami at age fifteen, he came face-to-face with blatant racism. In one instance, he was delivering medicine to a house and went straight up to the front door, something no Black person was expected or allowed to do. The homeowner alerted the local KKK. When word of this got to Sidney's brother, with whom the boy was living, he realized that Sidney had to get out of town, and quickly. He fled to New York, lived in an orphanage for a time, enlisted in the US Army, and eventually attempted to join theater companies. Unfortunately, his lilting Bahamian burr, and his race, led directors to say things like "Stop wasting your time—get a job as a dishwasher."

For many of us, such tribulations might have led to despair, or worse. Not for Sidney Poitier. He always felt that something better was coming; and this has been true of millions of Black people since slavery. A lot of the men and women I knew growing up had this feeling: they prayed for me, worked to help me, because they knew that faith was the only way forward, as it had been for them in much more trying circumstances than the ones in which I found myself.

Poitier is a perfect example of expecting and remaining open to better times. He didn't turn his many setbacks into self-pity; he simply forged ahead. He would go on to be many things beyond an Oscar-winning, groundbreaking actor—he would be the Bahamian ambassador to Japan, for example. But when, in 1964, Sidney became the first Black actor to win the Academy Award for his role in *Lilies of the Field*, he managed to teach Americans more about race than almost anyone. In the years that followed, he starred in a whole raft of incredibly important movies that showed the struggle that Black people faced every day in this country.

None of this would have been possible if he hadn't raised himself up, grasped every opportunity with both hands. But there's also this: Sidney knew about the magical universe, a place where things happen beyond our understanding. As he once told Oprah, he had been a sickly baby, and his mother had despaired of him surviving (he was born two months prematurely in Miami, before his family moved to the Bahamas). In that despair, Evelyn, his mother, took him to see a fortune teller, who said, "Don't worry about your son. He will not be a sickly child. He will walk with kings. He will step on pillars of gold. And he will carry your name to many places."

In reference to his mother, Sidney told Oprah that he "had that woman on my shoulder all my life. . . . She has been there taking care of me. I am not a hugely religious person, but I believe that there is a oneness with everything. And because there is this oneness, it is possible that my mother is the principal reason for my life."

I, too, am aware of the blessings of a strong mother.

+ + +

My mom, Jacqueline Alberta Gray, was the youngest of five kids—four girls and a boy. Her father, Leon, was a manager at an extermination company, and her mother, Zella, was a businesswoman who worked for Bulova. Zella was often the person who sold the most watches in the catalog—she was always moving up.

Mom got straight A's in school, loved reading, loved writing. She grew up in the Jamaica neighborhood of Queens, New York, but spent every summer in Virginia with her grandmother Betty. (The family had originated in Virginia and had moved north.) Mom attended Queens College and was a phlebotomist at New York City Hospital for a period.

Throughout much of that time, she attended debutante school, too. Zella was smart and recognized that her daughter Jacqueline was beautiful and could model and make a little extra money. But Zella also wanted my mother to be able to move through society—she didn't want my mom to be simply the girl from Queens who was born on the kitchen table.

My mother's parents split when she was ten, and she remained very close to her father, who died of a sudden heart attack when my mother was sixteen. Mom grew up in a three-level townhouse with extended family above and below her. With a very mixed background, her parents often passed for Italians.

The greatest gift my grandfather gave my mom was to have her become a pen pal. He'd read something in the paper about writing to kids in Europe and around the world, and he thought it would be good for my mother to do. "This is the way you get to know people," he said, "and maybe one day you'll meet one of them." Initially she thought it was a ridiculous idea, but eventually it worked to broaden her horizons from the busy streets of Queens. It gave her that spirit of always wanting to learn something about other people, always loving and appreciating someone else's culture, their background and experiences. I think that same spirit explains why she got involved in so many philanthropic efforts later in life: she had a passion for people, for broadening her own experience beyond that of just Beverly Hills or wherever she found herself.

It didn't hurt that she was an avid writer, and a talented one. She loved writing poetry, and as I've said, in another universe she could have been a writer or editor. I still have her writings from her student days; in her 1957 yearbook, for which she served as editor-in-chief, she wrote, "With God in our heart and a clear mind, our journey should steer straight and find happiness in the end." Her way of saying "Think you'll be happy" all the way back in the 1950s? Of course it was!

Mom often turned to writing to process loss and suffering (as I am doing here). I have a copy of her poem "Wrecked Faith," written at the age of seventeen after the death of her father. In it, she imagines sailors in a storm, facing heavy waves that "hurtle and surge." "Their souls are heavily oppressed," she writes, "and their flesh shivers as if unsecured." All feelings that I, too, have faced in the last two terrible years.

Later, Jacqueline Gray would be elected editor-in-chief of the 1960 yearbook in the Medical Technical Department at New York City Community College in Brooklyn, no small feat back then. (In those days, the yearbook was *everything* at a school or college—so much so that her elevation to the position was covered in numerous newspapers, including the *New York Daily News*.) I look at the yellowed clippings now, and a strong, serene, beautiful, undaunted face looks back at me. She was always a force, even when so much younger. "'All good things come in small packages,' say all who know Ms. Jacqueline Gray," one blurb begins. "Jackie," it goes on, "a petite young lady, gives the impression of being rather shy, but it takes no time at all for her warm personality to shine through."

At some point, Zella wanted that warm personality to be seen by everyone. She walked into my mother's bedroom one morning, woke her up, and told her there was a modeling contest that she figured Jacquie could win. This was noteworthy to my mother, because Zella was a busy woman: she was often employee of the week, month, and year—she got promoted all the time, and with five kids at home, attention was at a premium. Accordingly, my mother was always grasping for Zella, so when she told my mother that she thought she could win the contest, my mother gave her full attention and intention.

My mother didn't win that Miss Beaux Arts contest—rumor has it that she came in third—but it nevertheless served as an opening to an entire new world, a world in which Clarence Avant was already thriving. Recently, I was looking through some boxes and found a picture of my mother with Gig Young and Betsy von Furstenberg—that was the kind of world in which she found herself. She and Clarence first met on a bright, bright, sunshiny day in 1965 through their mutual friends Johnny and Sissy Nash (Johnny Nash of "I Can See Clearly Now" fame). My parents went on a couple of dates, but nothing much came of it.

Fate would reunite them in 1967, and something did

indeed happen—my mom became pregnant with me! They were married in New York on August 5, 1967, and I was born the following year in Los Angeles on my mother's birthday, March 6.

That shared birthday added to our very deep connection. But the fact that she got pregnant out of wedlock in 1967 was really something, too—not to mention the fact that she failed to tell my father, when he announced that they would be moving to Los Angeles, that she'd been on an airplane once before—on a trip to Spain with a fellow student!

When Mom arrived on the West Coast, she knew no one; but you could drop her into any fishbowl, and she would swim. This is another example of what I mean about raising yourself up. My mother's need for her own mother didn't disable her drive; she didn't dwell on the lack of attention. In our current world, the "sins" of parents seem to have become a catch-all for the inertia and poor behavior of the following generation—but for my parents' generation, those failings were fuel for betterment, not resentment. Sure, there were people in that later generation who went the way of evil because of the terrible things they'd suffered at the hands of cruel or inattentive parents, but more likely, such moments were used as motivation to create a better world, one not tainted by past traumas. As I mentioned earlier, my father was so badly treated by his stepfather that he tried to poison the older man—an extreme measure for an extreme wrong—but the abuse he was subjected to didn't lead to a life of anger and violence for Clarence. Instead, my father decided to better himself, to make something of his life, to be open to being mentored and open to learning, and—like Poitier and so many other self-made people—to grasp opportunities even when they seemed far-fetched or impossible.

Being open to the magical universe is everything. I'm not sure my father would put it that way, but I'm sure he'd agree that when we close ourselves off, when we decide that this is as far as we can go, when we say, "Nah, not for me—what if . . . ?" then we're guaranteeing that nothing will ever change, nothing will ever get better. Bottom line: nothing will come of nothing.

That doesn't mean we're tasked with puffing ourselves up. Every opportunity we throw ourselves into needs to be pursued from a position of gratitude and self-effacement, not from arrogance. "Let nothing be done through selfish ambition or conceit, but in lowliness of mind let each esteem others better than himself," advises the apostle Paul in Philippians 2:3. I think about my mother, yearning for love from Grandma Zella, yearning perhaps for a writer's life, a woman who got dropped into a distant city knowing no one and with a new baby—and from there, she created a rich and fulfilling life without recourse to self-pity. She didn't think the world owed her anything; she made herself out of isolation and modesty, and never let her ego and her missed opportunities create a sense of resentment at the world.

◆ ◆ ◆

The effects of all this could sometimes be seen in how my mother parented me.

When I was around twenty-five years old, my mother and I got to talking. She'd been reading Louise Hay's *You Can Heal Your Life* and had taken to heart the idea that we should watch our thoughts and be more mindful of the people around us. She asked me if there was anything I could think of that I felt I should forgive her for.

I almost said, rather glibly, "Lots of things!" Instead, I thought for a long moment and then boiled those things down to this: "Well," I said, "I wanted you to pay a little more attention to me."

She simply rolled her eyes in response. But I barreled on. "Whenever I went to a sleepover at someone's house, I noticed how their parents would tuck my friends in and tell them that they loved them, that kind of thing. And honestly, Mom, there were always so many people at our house, and you and Dad were always so busy supporting everyone around you, that I feel like I had to fight for any leftover attention and affection." I realize now that I was parroting how she probably felt about her own mother, Zella, but that didn't make it any less real or painful for me to explain.

My mother waited a beat for the dust to settle and then said, "Did I take you to school every day? Did I give you the birthday parties you dreamed of? Drive you everywhere you wanted to go? Make sure you had the best possible medical care? Didn't I make sure that you saw as much of the world as possible? Didn't I make you lunch every day? Didn't I read to you every night before you went to sleep?" Didn't I, didn't I, didn't I . . . The list went on and on.

I sat there in silence.

"Never mind," I eventually said. "This is a waste of time. I don't know why we're even trying to have a conversation about this. Why ask me if you didn't want to hear what I had to say?"

"I guess I could have—and *should* have—said the words 'I love you' more often," she said, "but that's just not who I am. To me, love is a verb. I chose to show my love for you through my actions."

◆ ◆ ◆

It would take years for us to come back to this conversation and make things right, but even in those intervening years, when things were unresolved, I still worked to cultivate a deep gratitude for what my parents had given me. Nonetheless, I spent so much time fixating on what emotions I *hadn't* gotten from them that I didn't fully honor the things they'd done (and were doing) for me. And that's always a waste of time.

Gratitude is an essential element of our experience of life, because we have no choice but to live the good and the bad, the ups and the downs. Given that there's no escaping the darker parts of life, our only hope is to live in gratitude for *all* of it; otherwise, we run the risk of living in resentment. We all hope to not have tribulations, but the one thing that my grandmother always drilled into me was a passage from the Gospel According to John (16:33). Jesus, knowing that all of us (himself included) would face hard times, said, "In the world you will have tribulation; but be of good cheer, I have overcome the world." Trials and tribulations are the one guarantee in life: every single person gets hammered in one way or another—or many. The loss of a child, a painful divorce, illness, violence . . . you can never know what it's going to be; you're just thrown into the arena, and you do the best you can. Given all that, it's exactly as my grandmother said: we have to always find the blessing, to *be* the blessing, and to always "play the glad game," as she put it. This game involves tricking your brain, because your brain follows whatever you give it. If you tell your brain you're glad, eventually you *will* be glad. (In other words, "Think you'll be happy.") Try it. Start directing your conscious mind, and you'll discover that the subconscious will listen and perform to your amazement. The subconscious will deliver the message you give it. Every. Single. Time. It will truly follow its orders.

When this terrible thing happened to my mom, my first thought was "God, what is good about this? I don't know one thing."

I took a moment, along with several deep breaths, and then I started to let my brain lead me. I'm grateful that my mom was extremely healthy throughout her life; that she lived with joy in her heart; that she had lots of friends, all over the world, all of whom adored her. I'm grateful that she got to visit her beloved Japan numerous times. I'm grateful that she showed me what the joy of living looks like.

We have to always find the blessing, to *be* the blessing.

Thank God my dad's still here with us; thank God we lived in town at the time my mom died and could get to him; thank God we're able to take care of him. And not only am I able to take care of him, I work from home, so I get to wake up and have breakfast with him and I get to have dinner with him every night and I'm blessed with the opportunity to nurture him back into some sense of sanity, and love him as a ninety-one-year-old needs to be loved—gently.

This gratitude stuff isn't about being delusional—it's about acknowledging that life can be hard, and not letting that difficulty define us and make us unable to see the joy and the upsides.

◆ ◆ ◆

There's a faction in our world now that says we're all owed something.

When the world doesn't deliver (though I would argue that the world is delivering all the time—we just have to be open to seeing what it's offering), then it's all too easy to fall into the trap of self-hatred. The magic of self-worth is, in fact, the truest form of modesty: knowing what we can and cannot do, and being open to what energy the world is sending us, liberates us into being effective in business and life. No, maybe we won't be astronauts; but the fact that we didn't get to stand on the moon doesn't mean we can't make the world a better place.

I fully understand how lucky I am to have been surrounded by a wide range of successful people in my life. Even though those people, with their impressive skills and accomplishments, were sometimes intimidating and often made me question my own abilities, I really had no other choice than to step up when called. I was all too aware that my parents had been raised in a very different country from the one that I was lucky to inherit. They and their friends had faced unimaginable roadblocks to success.

I'm just a few generations from slavery and a few years from legal segregation. What am I to do with that legacy?

Would I manage to be open to what the world is offering me?

Would I choose to show up when called?

Would I strive to live a life of gratitude for all the people who came before me and didn't get to do the things I get to do?

I know the answer to the questions above: we owe our ancestors this. And as a woman, I'm well aware that in many parts of the world females are looked down upon as second-class citizens, as less than, which is why we're overachieving in so many areas of life and culture. Women have been unseen for ages, a state that is the cruelest thing. (As Ralph Ellison so brilliantly described in his novel *Invisible Man*, being neglected, ignored, and unseen can be painfully debilitating.)

Take the singer-songwriter Bill Withers, as an example of someone who acknowledged and addressed the debt we owe our ancestors. One of the things Bill taught me was that you never know what's coming—you just have to be ready. There's nothing worse than praying for something and yet not being ready for it. Opportunities will *always* show up, and the great people among us are always ready.

Bill had been repeatedly told by music executives that they didn't hear a hit in his music; but he kept persevering. He was working as an airplane mechanic, but he'd already written "Lean on Me." Imagine knowing you've written a seminal, classic song like "Lean on Me," but you're being constantly told that it's not a hit. (Can you imagine what kind of deal with the devil any songwriter would make now to write something as great as that song?)

What did my father see and hear in Bill that nobody else did? It wasn't "Ain't No Sunshine," or even "Lean on Me"—it was the song "Grandma's Hands" that captured

> **You never know what's coming— you just have to be ready.**

my father's imagination. It echoed what Dad always says: "What do all of us have and how did we all get here? Through our grandmothers." And the song came from such a profound place for Bill—his grandmother, Gracchus Monroe Galloway, had been born an enslaved person, and he'd watched her in church joyfully singing and clapping, using those hands that would sometimes "ache . . . and swell." He honored his ancestors; he honored them by being ready.

So, like the many examples put before me, I learned that it was important to always be ready.

COBB SALAD

I wake to the smell of bacon. Weird—I didn't think Ted was cooking today.

Each waking after a loss is a new moment of pain, a new beginning to the end: you come slowly out of dark dreams, and your eyes focus on the ceiling, on the walls, and your mind zeroes in on what's missing, what's changed.

As with every day, I started that day by praying for divine intelligence, praying for divine order, praying for divine wisdom. By *divine* I mean belonging to something bigger than myself. So divine intelligence is knowledge beyond my learning; divine order is an act of giving myself over to something that might feel uncomfortable, but that is part of a greater plan; divine wisdom is the chance to tap into the energy of my ancestors and betters, those whose experience and insight will always outrun my own.

And I pray for this: divine correction when I need to be corrected. When something I've said or done doesn't land right, what is my responsibility to make things better?

Even before my mother's death, I sensed that I'd begun to give away a lot of my power, making way for divine wisdom to assert itself. I was sure I knew what I wanted to do in almost every situation, but I made a point of checking myself and asking others for their opinions—basically, I started trusting myself less, which was actually liberating. I started to always look for a sign. I was looking for peace about things, and when I didn't feel at peace, that in itself was the sign that I should change tack. Perhaps my ego wanted something, but my soul was saying, "Just wait." This perspective seeped out into the whole of my life; if I felt someone was an energy vampire, I questioned what I was giving away to that person and why. My joy became my power, and I needed to share that joy only with those who were going to appreciate it. If I was loving a project but not liking the people who were involved in the project, did I have to tough it out, given that life is so damn short?

I remember one magazine calling and inviting me to join a roundup of badass women (their description). I prayed for divine intelligence, order, wisdom, *and* correction on that one! And what I felt was, women need to learn how to be noble and kind and get back to the basics of life. We have been blessed with the gift of the divine feminine, which is *not* a negative. On the contrary, women have a special connection with the spiritual realm. We've been given the blessing of bringing souls into the world, so we bear a heavy responsibility for nurturing those souls. Being genuinely feminine (meaning being a multitasker, an intuitive, a problem-solver, an empath, a person who inspires) was one of my mother's superpowers—she truly loved being alive. She always rose above the negative and the unnecessary.

I'm not sure why we now often consider raising kids or running a household or supporting our partner—things my mother excelled at and extolled the virtues of—negatives. So I'm all for women being badasses, but there's a balance to be achieved. If you're a badass and you have a kid who's bullying other kids at school, what does that say about you? Doesn't sound very badass to me. It's actually pretty pathetic. Do you want to be the bad badass or do you want to raise your kid to not be an asshole? The badass should be the icing, not the cake.

+ + +

Donnie Smith—Joe Smith's widow—and her daughter, Julie, were two of our first visitors after Mom's death. That afternoon, we sat around the table eating the delicious Cobb salad that had been made by Gwyneth with such love and care. Donnie, as usual, looked fabulous—like my mother, Donnie never left home

without looking like she was ready to walk a red carpet—
but I could tell she was shell-shocked, too. Then, in the
middle of the meal, Donnie's stoicism, so prevalent in
that generation (my mother had it in spades—they all
did), simply crumbled.

"Somebody hurt my friend," she wailed, over and over.
"I can't believe someone did this to my friend."

Eventually, she calmed down and whispered to
my father, "Wow, this Gwyneth can really cook—I'm
impressed!"

♦ ♦ ♦

People just kept coming over, kept bringing their beauty
and love and memories of Jacqueline Avant—my
kindergarten friends, high-school friends, college friends,
everyone. My high-school friends, especially, brought
great comfort because they'd spent so much time with
my mom. Our house had been the one kids came to, to
hang out; everyone was welcome.

And Mom's friends came too, of course, loyal even
beyond the grave.

Way back in the early seventies, a few years after
my parents moved to LA, my mother dropped me off

at nursery school one day, alone as usual. She herself was pretty much alone all the time then; she was a transplanted New Yorker, and LA is a very different place.

So there was Jacqueline Avant, standing by herself, looking through the gates at me toddling up to the school door. Also there that day, at some distance, were two other women—Adrienne and Elaine—who had likewise just moved from New York. All three mothers were waiting and watching their children (me, Cece, and Ross) to make sure we all made friends with each other and weren't going to run back to our mothers.

Adrienne said, "Look at that lady over there. She's by herself."

"Let's invite her for coffee," Elaine replied.

From that day on the three women were inseparable best friends. They celebrated every single birthday together—they didn't miss one year. And when this tragedy showed up, so did they. I was proud that I, too, now seemed to have a similar gang of ride-or-dies.

One of my biggest fears was that my mom's extended family and friends would learn about her death from the news. In some ways, the friends you choose are even more dear than the family you're dealt by God. But how was I going to tell these folks what had happened? My mom's sister, Jean, just shy of ninety—how could I tell her? And my cousin Brian? How could I tell him? Her friends Adrienne and Elaine, too—I'd have to call them. And her dear friend, and my godmother, Audrey, who, when I reached her and told her, wailed in despair with her partner, Gail.

What had happened, and the need to spread the word, was beyond overwhelming. I could feel the world closing in on me; I felt as if I were drowning in quicksand.

My friend Susana—who leads the news team for RNZ, a leading New Zealand radio station, and thus had heard the news early, even at great distance—got me on the phone, in between my meetings with the detectives and organizing my father's clothes in his new closet at my home. We could speak only briefly, so she got right to the point. She said, very sternly, "I'm sending candles, crystals, and Samoan prayers. The prayers are already there; the candles and crystals will be there in two weeks. But listen: whatever you do right now, do *not* google your mom or yourself. This awful thing happened; it's real. It's a top-ten international news story. Instead, what I need you to do is get in the water, Nicole. Get in the bath. Now. Ground. Ground. Ground. You must ground yourself. Salt, lavender oil, and prayer."

Think You'll Be Happy

And I listened and got grounded.

And once I was grounded, I picked up the phone and dialed. And then I told Adrienne and Elaine about Jacqueline Avant. I had no divine wisdom in those calls. Some things are beyond all understanding.

SIX

Raise Yourself Up

Jacquie could sense when you were having
problems. Whether it was a physical issue,
or financial or something mental, like
a big breakup or a breakdown, Jacquie
would pick up the phone, call you, and
ask, "How are you doing?" If, like most
of us, you first acknowledged that you
were just fine, Jacquie would quietly wait,
knowing her senses had not deceived her.

My mom loved people who walked the walk; she admired and respected visionaries, people who tried new
things, people who put themselves on the line and did things
that others said couldn't be done. One day, as I was going

through my mother's things, I found various articles on Oprah Winfrey, Bobby Shriver, and Ted. It was especially moving to me because I knew why: to my mom, these were people changing the world in very big ways. Bobby with his RED movement, physically saving lives around the world; Oprah spiritually saving lives everywhere she went; and Ted's company sharing stories that would entertain, educate, and inspire the human spirit, especially when we all needed it most during COVID. It was no coincidence that they all would hold me up that month of December and beyond.

(Oprah and I would laugh about all those clippings, but she understood how emotional that moment was for me, too—powerful, hard to bear with my mother gone, but healing, all at the same time.)

I remember thinking, as I reflected about my mom and her respect for people who got out and changed the world, about Bill Withers and his tenacity. It's legend now that he was making aircraft toilets when my father "discovered" him, but there's much more to it than that. Yes, he was an aircraft mechanic, but while working that perfectly respectable job, he wrote "Lean on Me," "Ain't No Sunshine," and "Grandma's Hands." Those songs didn't come *after* he became famous; they were written *before*. His fame could never have happened if Bill hadn't been ready, and if my father hadn't been open to his genius. To accomplish big things, to change the world, you have to see the magic in the moment and take what it offers you—in Bill's case, being ready—because you never know when your name is going to get called.

I thought, too, of Barack Obama and the legion of people who worked to get him elected to the White House, hoping to change the world. A better world was certainly *my* hope when I joined the campaign. By getting involved and making connections and raising ourselves up, we raised a ton of money for the future president, but more important, we changed the political dynamic of the United States. By 2020, you could look at a Democratic primary debate and barely notice (but also *really* notice) that it featured Black, white, Asian, Latino, straight, gay, female, male, all together on the podium, hashing out a vision for America that is inclusive, and real, and the future. We had raised ourselves up without having to rely on the usual methods. We had taken control. Oh, and on January 20, 2009, Barack Hussein Obama was inaugurated as the forty-fourth president of the United States. (So much for the crazy name, huh Dad?)

◆ ◆ ◆

After my mom died, there were many times I couldn't fully put my arms around what had happened. But I knew I had to move forward. I would look in the mirror in the mornings and say, "This really did happen. This is your new reality. This is a new moment. You're gonna have to figure it out as you go along, because you've never experienced something so cataclysmic before. And you don't know anybody who has."

"Okay, God," I'd say, "All right, universe—here we go. Here's a new day. Lead me to whatever I need to do. Send me people who are stronger than I am, who can give me some wisdom, who can give me comfort."

There were days that I asked only for comfort. There were days that I asked only for strength. There were days that I asked only for clarity. There were days that I just wanted to sleep and turn the world off. (Hat tip to Xanax.) I was so far out of my comfort zone . . . but I'd been out there. I knew how to turn things around. I knew how to function. So that's what I did: I ditched the Xani, and I went back to work.

◆ ◆ ◆

Once Barack Obama became President Obama, I knew he planned to nominate me for an ambassadorship. Initially I thought I'd ask to go to Barbados. I thought it was important to head to a Black country: I wanted Black people to see a Black woman in a position of power, representing a Black president and in a Black nation.

But one day Sidney Poitier called me and invited me to lunch, to his legendary booth in the back of Spago in Beverly Hills. Sidney had been the Bahamian ambassador to Japan for a decade, and for some reason, I couldn't think of a better person to tell all about my plans . . . for *Barbados*.

Before I'd gotten very far, Sidney said, "Have you thought about the Bahamas? There's great need there, too, and you'd be perfect."

The country known as the Bahamas—sitting out there in the Atlantic about one hundred miles off the coast of Florida—is a series of many disparate islands. It has its fair share of poverty and prejudice, not to mention a drug-trafficking problem and illegal immigration and the attendant and intractable issue of refugees. The more Sidney talked, the more a Bahamian ambassadorship felt like a challenge I wanted to rise to. I thought about my mother taking on the challenge of Watts; she didn't know what she was getting into, only that there was a need and she was being called to service. This is the nature of service: to not ask what could go wrong or right, but simply to step up when called.

By the end of the lunch, the Bahamas was more and more seeming like the right place for me, so I was delighted when the president agreed.

But first, I had to convince the body politic that I was the right person for the job.

This is the nature of service: to step up when called.

As I studied and met with various senators and other leaders in Washington leading up to my Senate confirmation hearing, something magical happened: an African man who served as a bellhop/valet at my hotel told me that he and his colleagues had been praying regularly for me. Then, on the day of the actual hearing, one of the Black janitors said to me, "Go get 'em girl—I'm praying for you. I've been here a long time—it feels so good watching you walk through these halls."

With that in mind, I felt invincible.

In my remarks before the Senate Foreign Relations Committee, I wanted to highlight why it was so important to me to heed Barack Obama's call to serve—and why my ancient and recent history was leading me to this work:

North Carolina is where my father was born in 1931 and where the seeds of hard work, big dreams, and pure ethics were planted in my character. My father left home at the age of fourteen to escape the evils of the Jim Crow South. He never received a formal education, but because of his values, he rose to become chairman and leader of several major companies and a trusted advisor to leaders in media, politics, business, and civil rights. My mother and father instilled in me the values of hard work, service to others, and respect and honor for all men and women without prejudice.

Both Democrats *and* Republicans were positive about my nomination, until I got a call one day as I landed back at LAX airport.

Apparently, one Democratic senator was threatening to not vote for me because he hadn't gotten a meeting with me when I'd been in DC. The first thing I did after hearing this was to call my dad, in tears. "I may not become an ambassador because somebody has something against me—and I can't believe that that somebody is from my own party," I wailed.

Now, other times that I've called my dad crying, he's simply said, "It is what it is" and hung up. My dad is full of one-liners like that: "It is what it is—what are you going to do about it?" "If you don't ask, you don't get." "Live every day as if it were your last, because someday you're gonna be right." Even now, at each breakfast we share, I'll be bemoaning something I've read in the paper or seen on TV, and he'll just say, "Hey, listen, nothing remains the same." So back then I was expecting another one-liner from Dad.

He surprised me. This was one of the relatively few times that I've heard my dad be extremely patient on the other end of the line and really let me cry something out.

Finally he said, "Nicole, you have to keep the faith."

Easier said than done, Dad.

I said, "They want me to go back to DC tomorrow," as though they'd asked me to donate a kidney or drown a puppy or something.

Clarence said, "You're going. I'll get you the ticket. This is a great opportunity, and sometimes shit just shows up."

This was a man who'd overcome so much; he didn't belabor that point, ever, but I could hear in his voice that he understood what a setback felt like. His response? Face it; fight it; make the future, don't mourn the past. And don't ever let low self-esteem block an opportunity. Low self-esteem is just another form of narcissism anyway, as though your self-doubt could or should be fixed by some vast, cosmic force that sees the real you. I thought of Matthew 6:34: "Therefore do not worry about tomorrow, for tomorrow will worry about its own things. Sufficient for the day is its own trouble." I couldn't control what was going to happen in DC; I just had to get on the plane and find out.

The next day, as I flew east, I talked silently to myself the whole way. "You know what?" I thought, "I'm standing on the shoulders of four hundred years of people who would never have dreamed that one day there would be a Black president, or even a Black ambassador to the Bahamas. But they never stopped believing freedom was around the corner, so who am I to not believe the same?" That brought to mind John 20:29: "Blessed are those who have not seen and yet have believed."

Sitting tall in my airplane seat, I felt that I had that authority, too, because I'd never prayed so hard in my life; I was determined to walk into that office with a sturdy armor of faith around me, the armor of prayer and of self-worth that comes from knowing that you're called at the behest of something bigger than your own ego—in my case, called by all those faces peering at me through the fog of the past, through all those years of pain and suffering. Again a scripture passage came to mind, Psalm 31:24: "Be of good courage, and He shall strengthen your heart, all you who hope in the Lord."

Honestly, by the time I landed in DC, I didn't even care if the senator in question said no. "Whatever happens," I thought, as the wheels touched down, "I have the authority."

It also helped that I also had a metaphorical weapon in my back pocket.

But first, the senator had to try to rattle me. "Nice to meet you," he said, shaking my hand. "I just need to find out about you. You're an actress, yes?"

"What are you talking about?" I said.

"Well, my team told me that you were *just an actress*." This was going to be even more fun than I'd expected.

"I was on *Sesame Street* when I was six," I said, very calmly. "I've done three commercials in my life and did a couple of TV shows to pay bills, as so many others do in LA. I even tried out for Will Smith's love interest in *The Fresh Prince of Bel-Air*, but they picked Tyra Banks because, well, she's *Tyra Banks*."

Don't get me wrong, there's nothing bad about being an actress—but I wasn't *just* an actress.

The senator looked like he'd seen a ghost.

"I'm actually a businesswoman," I further clarified. "I'm the vice president of a music publishing company, and I've been working solidly since I was ten years old."

I then went through every single job, which honestly was overkill but enormous fun.

And then I pulled out my secret weapon: "And we've already met, Senator, when I was working for Harold Ford Jr. Harold had told me that you're a really good man, and that we should raise money for you. You and I met at my friend Michael's law firm in Beverly Hills. We had a luncheon—remember? It started a little before 12:30 p.m., and ended just after 2:00, and I raised money for your election campaign." There was nothing more satisfying than actually remembering the exact time of the luncheon.

The senator heartily recommended my nomination, no more questions asked.

At that moment, I'd become not only an ambassador for my country, but also an ambassador for my own life; I'd stood up for myself, and for the fact that this was not about me, but about the causes that Sidney Poitier and others had alerted me to, and about the needs of the Bahamian people.

But there was something else, too, another lesson from my ancestors that I leaned on in those days (and still do). That lesson was this: I had to put aside my needs to concentrate on the needs of others. My paternal grandmother always used to say to me, if I ever complained about anything (she hated complaining), "Sweetheart, if everyone in the world came into the room and put their problems on a table, and you put yours on the same table, and everyone got to choose, I promise you you'd grab your own problems back pretty darned quickly once you saw what everyone else had to deal with. You'd have people saying they don't have a toilet, or a refrigerator, or a mom or a dad, or food to eat, or even somewhere to lay their head at night."

I didn't fully appreciate what she meant when I was younger. I thought, "Can't I just vent once in a while? Can we not have an effing lesson for every effing thing?" (I'm sorry—but not—to say that Ted's kids say the same thing to me all the time.) But now I get it. I needed to change the level of my joy so that I could appreciate how lucky I was and always had been.

There were lessons everywhere when I was growing up. In our house my mother created what we called the Great Wall, featuring photos of Frederick Douglass, Booker T. Washington, Marcus Garvey, George Washington Carver, Adam Clayton Powell Jr., James Baldwin, Paul Robeson, Harriet Tubman, Black abolitionists, artists, writers, scientists, and politicians we admired; slave papers (yes, an actual copy of a transaction); oh, and Alexandre Dumas (he's only half Black, but since he wrote two of her favorite novels, *The Three Musketeers* and *The Count of Monte Cristo*, my mom allowed him on the wall). Mom would say, "It's not just to inspire you and encourage you—it's to help you understand that you weren't the first with everything. You're not the first; you're not the greatest."

Every time I was described as the first African American female to go to the Bahamas as ambassador, my mother would say, "Frederick Douglass was the first African American nominated for vice president of the United States, and the first Black consul general to Haiti. That was 1889. I mean, really!"

If ever I was tempted to worry about being outside my comfort zone, all I had to do was think about Frederick

Douglass, about him putting his problems on a table with mine, and whose problems I'd rush to grab.

Oh, and don't let anyone call you "just an actress." In fact, don't let anyone call you "just" anything.

◆ ◆ ◆

From my earliest age, Mom would always put me into situations and places and let me observe and learn for myself, however uncomfortable that might make me; she didn't lecture, she just *did*.

> Don't let anyone call you "just" anything.

One summer afternoon when I was quite young, she picked me up from summer camp, but instead of turning north into the Trousdale Estates, she kept heading west, eventually landing us smack in the middle of UCLA. Without saying much, she marched us to the top of the bleachers in the blazing sun, sat herself down, got out some lunch, and waited.

Seating myself beside her, I was confused. What was she up to this time? "Mom . . . ?" I prompted.

"Nicole, we're going to watch these athletes run," she said, handing me a sandwich.

Down on the track, athletes were warming up and then sprinting—but something seemed different, unusual.

"What's wrong with *him?*" I said to my mom, pointing out one of the young men on the track. "Why is he running so slowly?"

"Let's just watch them," she said.

After a while, she took me down to the pool to watch swimmers train. Once again, I couldn't work out what I was supposed to think. The swimming wasn't as fast as what I'd seen on TV.

As I started to once again question what I was seeing, Mom stopped me. "Nicole," she said, "this is the Special Olympics. These are athletes like you and your friends, some faster or slower or whatever. What matters is that they're *trying*. They may look different and behave differently from you and me, but they're actually the same. They're competing. Just like you compete every day at camp. They may run slower than the athletes we tend to see on TV, but they'd still beat most of us! So yes, they might sound different when they talk and they might look different, but their hearts aren't different. They're *people*, competing to win."

And that's one of the greatest gifts she gave me: to point out the value of people without ever lecturing me. She would simply put me in a situation and let me assess it—and as a child will, I often missed the point!—and then she'd kindly correct me, if need be, as she did there in Westwood as those Special Olympians excelled at their chosen sports.

One night, my parents had a small dinner party for some friends of theirs and I noticed two of the men were holding hands—this was in the early 1980s. I had never seen two men hold hands before—it was a different time—so I ran into the kitchen.

"Dad!" I said. "Did you see them in the dining room? They're holding hands!"

My father, like Mom that day at UCLA, didn't say anything. Instead, he had me pick up a platter to take to the dining room.

On my return, he said, "Well, I guess they like each other." Later he added, "People have been gay since the beginning of time, Nicole. Get over it."

What I was learning through all this was that I was not to focus on differences; but instead I was to find common ground wherever I could, with whomever I could. I was raised in a privileged world, but my parents were going to be damned if it made me privileged. My father's upbringing had been poverty-stricken; my mother's family were a little better off, but she and her siblings had also grown up in a world where opportunities weren't handed to anyone.

What I was being trained to be was the ambassador for my own character. We all need to be the ambassadors for our own lives. Think of yourself as a country, and think about what that country believes in. What are the values of that place? What's your "constitution"? What are your borders? Who gets to come in? Does that person bring a positive energy, a soul that looks outward, not inward?

This isn't just some metaphysical idea. It has practical applications at any age and for anyone.

Years ago, one of my mom's friends got me involved in a program at the University of Southern California called Neighborhood Academic Initiative, a seven-year college-prep program for students from south and east Los Angeles.

When I showed up to volunteer, the director of the program and I couldn't pin down how best I might contribute, until I made an observation toward the end of our meeting. "The one thing I did notice about your students," I said, "was that there's no way I would hire any of them to work for me. No one looked up; no one looked me in the eye when they shook my hand. And they all seemed kind of negative."

I watched a light bulb go off above the director's head. "Really?" he said. "So what do you suggest?"

Considering his question, I thought about what my mother had learned in debutante school: how to present herself to a hostile world so that people didn't see only a young Black woman, but also saw someone who was ready to move ahead, ready to go places. I also thought about my earlier musings on being your own ambassador, about how crucial that is if you're going to get ahead in the world.

My mom has been described as a shining, living example of elegance, which is perfectly captured here as she celebrated her eightieth birthday at Spago in Beverly Hills. *Stefanie Keenan*

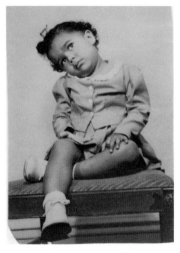

My mother in 1943. She remembered saying, "Hurry up, my neck's hurting."

My mother with her father, Leon Gray, in Queens in 1943. My mother was the youngest of five children; she and her father were very close. He died, sadly, when she was seventeen.

My mother with Grandma Betty in Virginia, summer 1948. Betty was born into chattel slavery; she urged her grandchildren to be hardworking, forward-looking, and open to everything the world had to offer.

My mother in 1962; she was twenty-two years old. Here seen in New York City being admired while competing for the Miss Beaux Arts title. *Irving Overby*

Jacqueline Gray, front and center. Behind her is my godmother, Audrey Smaltz, another powerhouse; they met at the legendary Ophelia DeVore School of Self-Development and Modeling. (Audrey remembers that Jacquie burst into tears when she didn't win Miss Beaux Arts; Audrey just punched her and said, "Don't you dare cry!") *Courtesy of the Jacqueline Avant Estate*

Me with my parents in 1971 in Beverly Hills. *Weldon McDougal*

My mother and father, Clarence Avant, with Lena Horne in 1966. My parents married a year later, and I came along pretty soon after.

My mother said that I was always pondering; this, therefore, was her favorite picture of me. *Weldon McDougal*

With Grandma Zella and my mom in 1972. My grandmother and I clearly liked checks.

My parents at my baby shower, with my godfather, Quincy Jones.

Legendary singer-songwriter Bill Withers—pictured here hugging me at his wedding reception at our home in Trousdale Estates in 1973. I was heartbroken; Bill was my first love.

The Great Cassius Clay had a lot to say when he signed for his bout with Sonny Liston, and Cassius was not speechless when he recently visited the Ophelia De Vore School of Charm and ....As if you didn't know, the poetry began to flow. During the impromptu visit, Cassius sat in on a Personality Class and took part in a question and answer session. The girls asking all the questions and turning on the charm are all students at the Ophelia De Vore School. No one was quite sure who was the more excited, the girls or Cassius Clay.

Boxing legend Cassius Clay, seen here surrounded by women from the Ophelia DeVore School, in the early 1960s. My mother is pictured bottom right. Later, Cassius—by that point Muhammad Ali—would be at our house all the time.

Muhammad Ali with my mother, me, and my brother, Alex, at our home in Trousdale Estates in 1992.

Me with Sir Sidney Poitier in his favorite booth at Spago in Beverly Hills, where he urged me to serve as ambassador to the Bahamas instead of Barbados. *Courtesy of the Jacqueline Avant Estate*

At a Young Business Leader fundraiser in Hollywood for Barack Obama's first presidential run, February 2007.

September 9, 2009, at the State Department in Washington, DC, at my swearing-in ceremony before becoming the US ambassador to the Bahamas. From left: my mom and dad; my brother, Alex; my husband, Ted Sarandos; Sarah Sarandos; my godmother, Audrey Smaltz; Tony Sarandos; then Secretary of State Hillary Clinton; and my aunt Anne Woods. *Courtesy of Ambassador Nicole Avant personal archives*

On a visit with Shaun Robinson to the Willie Mae Pratt Centre for Girls in Nassau, the Bahamas. This was one of the most meaningful days of my ambassadorship—there was no script, just me and Shaun and the girls sharing stories about our lives.

My mom with Adrienne and Elaine. The three of them became best friends after a chance meeting in 1971 while dropping off their children (me, Cece, and Ross) at nursery school.

Thanksgiving was always our favorite family holiday. Here we are all together, in 2021. This would be the last time I would ever see my mother.

My mom was my dad's lifeline—she kept him social and active. Here they are in 2019, at the premiere of the documentary we made about his life and career, *The Black Godfather*. *Mark Leibowitz/Netflix*

New Year's Day 2022 in Montecito. My father with me and Ted, and our friends Gwyneth, Brad, and Laura, who were insistent on restoring some sense of joy in what was still a very difficult, raw, and shocking time for my family and me.

My mom, making a wish, at our last birthday lunch together at the Polo Lounge—her favorite spot—in March 2021.

My own light bulb went off: "I'm thinking of a social behavior class," I said. "Maybe even something a bit metaphysical, about how words and talking affect your life, how your thoughts affect your life . . ."

On the first day of my actual participation, I spoke to a group of seventh-, eighth-, and ninth-graders, and then some high-school kids. Pretty early on, I was lucky to be challenged by a student, Joanna, who said, "It's really great that you want us to think positive, and it's really great that you're telling us every day that we could be anything we want, but we already know that. We don't really give a shit. We want to know *how.*"

Point taken. From that day forward I put my students into as many different situations as I could, and always out of their neighborhoods. I also had my friends and colleagues from various walks of life come and share their stories so that the students could see various new paths.

I, too, shared my story and expressed to them that the best training for me in life had been to step out of my comfort zone and learn new skills. Every job I'd had was a stepping stone to the next. I sold shoes—terrible at it. I waitressed—loved it. I worked in TV—loved that, too. I worked in the record business, and loved every single second. But just because I landed on my feet didn't mean that I wasn't paralyzed by fear whenever I started something new. I was always afraid that my employer would realize that I wasn't qualified and show me the door on my second or third day.

I told the students that the main lesson I'd learned by the time I was in my thirties was that no job was beneath me, and that I was not above anyone. Every job delivered new lessons, gave me opportunities to acquire new skill sets. I learned who I wanted to be and who I didn't want to be. This was especially true when I waited tables, because if you ever want to be truly humbled, be a server: you'll see the best and worst of human nature, often during the same shift.

This understanding of where I fit in the world—no better than, no worse than—was a great gift that my parents had given me.

◆ ◆ ◆

With Barack's example in mind, I went to the Bahamas to serve the country and him. I owed my, and his, ancestors this much; this was my way of expressing gratitude for all the people who came before me and didn't get to do such things, or even imagine them to be possible. If it meant going out of my comfort zone, then so be it.

It wasn't as if I were the first person to do something that felt uncomfortable. But my faith helped me deal with that discomfort. As 2 Timothy 1:7 reminds us, "For God has not given us a spirit of fear, but of power and of love and of a sound mind."

I was moving to the islands with a new husband—I'd married Ted Sarandos right before my job started—and my dog, Boshko. On the plane on the way out there, we (well, not *Boshko*) had discussed the initiatives I wanted to sponsor: in education, alternative energy, economic and small business development, and empowerment of and raising awareness about the challenges facing people with disabilities. In all those goals, I felt the gentle urgings of my mother's deepest passions.

◆ ◆ ◆

My mother always taught me to ask a simple but crucial question when I went to a new place: "Where's the orphanage?"

So that's what I did in the Bahamas.

My local staff were taken aback. "No ambassador has ever asked us that," they said. But it was ingrained in me. My mom was always asking, "Where are the orphans? Where are the foster kids? Where are the underserved? How can we serve?"

Early in my tour, Ted was coming to visit for Christmas and bringing his children, Tony and Sarah. (As I noted in an earlier chapter, I would come to consider them mine, too, even though they were the product of his previous marriage.) So I ordered a bunch of toys in the States and asked the kids—they were in their midteens at the time—and Ted to bring them on their visit to Nassau.

I did this for a couple of reasons. One, obviously, I wanted to go to the orphanages and take some Christmas cheer to kids who might otherwise go without; that's what my mother had ingrained in me. But she'd ingrained something else in me, too. I knew that when Tony and Sarah arrived in my new country, they'd be treated like royalty by the wonderful Bahamians. So a small part of what I was doing was grounding those lovely kids, just as my mother had always grounded me—and they responded wonderfully. Sarah wrapped every single present and baked cookies, and she and Tony enjoyed meeting the kids and handing out the gifts, sitting with those youngsters for ages while they all played and hung out.

I had a different approach generally to some other ambassadors. Whereas many of them focused on writing reports and doing the strategic work of intercountry politics, I wanted to show America in its best light in the Bahamas; and I wanted to bring some magic to the place so that people felt inspired to be their best selves.

But first, I wanted to get to know what our folks on the ground did, the Americans who worked out of the embassy and made the place safe for locals and tourists alike. I asked, for example, to go out with the US Coast Guard teams on some shifts. Though I was reading all their reports, those documents were so boring and bureaucratic that I wasn't learning much from them. I was done with staying comfortable. I wasn't facing down smugglers, God knows, but I was at least opening my experience to those who do.

This was the start of my really bonding with my so-called country team down there. I was determined to take the time to try to understand exactly what each of them went through daily. This seemed to me a key job of the ambassador: to be open enough to admit that she doesn't know enough, and then to learn. I already knew that the Bahamas was a magnet for drug dealing and illegal immigration; I also knew that that meant my guys in the Coast Guard had had to witness some really upsetting stuff. So I asked them directly about the deaths they'd seen—mothers and children drowning when their attempts at sneaking into the United States had gone horribly wrong. They were grateful that I cared (we should all care), and they admitted how harrowing the job can be. I also insisted on heading away from Nassau to see some of the more distant islands. (There are at least seven hundred islands and cays; not all of them are habitable, but each is unique.) On one trip we went to Inagua, way south (just off Cuba), where OPBAT (Operations Bahamas Turks and Caicos) is located. The place has mosquitoes the size of bats. No, seriously—I actually could feel the weight of them as they landed on me.

All it had taken was a willingness to be uncomfortable and to use that feeling to learn something; to be open to someone else's experience; to leave my ego at the door. I was representing my country and my president, so it was the least I could do to find out what the people on the ground needed, what they faced, what they felt. The way I did that was to *listen*.

Someone else's story is always more interesting than your own, in any case. Even when you think your life is fascinating, when you open up to someone else's experience, *that's* when true learning happens. All you have to do is shut up long enough to hear it. Because when you listen to someone, you're putting aside your comfort zone and stepping into an understanding of what others are facing. It's just like that big old table my grandmother used to talk about, covered in all the troubles of the world. When faced with the choice, would you pick someone else's, or pick up your own and get on with fixing them?

LAURA 3:52

On the day Laura and Candace arrived to see me, I think they expected to be turned away; my mother's death was too new. But I wasn't going to live by societal rules. Instead, I invited them in and gave them a choice of four jobs to do for me.

Laura and Candace went separately and together, all over the city, to find the best final resting place for Mom. For someone so orderly, it was notable that she'd never mentioned where she wanted to be laid to rest. I once asked her—adding, "And no, Mom, I'm not taking your ashes to Japan!"—but she simply said, "I haven't thought about it." I wonder now if that prospect was *too* final for her.

And that's why Laura and Candace found themselves heading to Santa Monica, to Montecito, to Forest Lawn in Griffith Park. Meanwhile, I was upstairs in our house, trying to get my father settled. What can you say to a man who's just lost his partner of fifty-four years, and in such a sudden and violent way.

Montecito was the prettiest possibility for a resting place, but I settled on Santa Monica; something about her being close for her friends to visit and being near the ocean just felt right. I was about to wire the money to a funeral home that they'd found when Ted unexpectedly said, "Remember the cemetery where our friend Leonard is buried? We should have Mom laid to rest there. It's beautiful and serene, and it's nondenominational."

We checked it out, and it was perfect. Her best friend Sandy is resting a few feet away, and so is another great friend, Nancy. It's not a coincidence to me that so many souls who were close to our family now rest close to each other.

In those early days I was still struggling with reality. It's a truism to say that nothing prepares a person for an unexpected loss, but it's worth saying all the same. The mind just can't wrap itself around something so vast and eternal. Language can't keep up. I think that's why the best condolences I received just sent love rather than trying to imagine or even describe what I was going through. Grief is the loneliest island; I knew my father's grief was a different one to my own, for example; I knew Ted's was different again; I knew my mother's friends felt things I would never understand, as they probably knew I was feeling a raft of things they couldn't fathom. I thought about my brother, his anger in the hospital as we waited for news that night; that, too, was a form of

grief—his pacing, his incendiary heart. That loneliness of
loss cannot be mitigated; it can only be acknowledged
and respected. So the best notes I got said just "I love
you" and then let the silence speak its volumes. Just to
allow for the silence was all I really needed.

But discovering that Mom could rest surrounded
by people she'd loved and who had loved her brought
me a new peace, a peace that I hadn't felt in days. I was
beginning to understand that there was every chance
that my mom was working from the other side. I was
being guided to where Mom must have wanted to be. The
universe and my mom were already working together.

All this was a great comfort to me; it convinced me, if
I needed any more convincing, that if one is open to the
universe, it delivers. And yet . . . still my mother wouldn't
come to me, wouldn't speak to me from beyond. She had
come to Ted (who never remembers his dreams); and
she was coming to my friend Laura, though—and I don't
know how else to put this—my mother didn't even know
Laura.

"She came to me last night at 3:33," Laura said
one day. Laura is the most honest person you could
ever find—the smartest, the kindest—so I know that
what she's telling me is true, and real, and should be
comforting . . . but still it hurts. Why Laura and not me?

"Mom," I say to her unseen self in exasperation, "you don't even know Laura. You're waking *her* and not *me*? Screw Laura!"

December rolled on. Life has a way of reasserting itself. I was learning just how famous my mother was; there were newspaper articles all over the world; people were writing, calling, texting. My mother was everywhere—everywhere, that is, except with me.

Eventually, the Christmas season was upon us all. I was dreading our first Christmas without Mom. I was keeping busy, preparing for the season, but still her absence nagged at me.

And then it was very early on the morning of Christmas Eve, and I couldn't get back to sleep. It was about 3:45 a.m. Without waking Ted and the dogs, I walked downstairs, deep in my own feelings, trying to understand how I could celebrate this season with such an emptiness. I walked through the dining room and remembered what a character my mother had been. I'd recently found a note that Sarah, Ted's daughter, had written to my mom for Mother's Day 2017.

"Thank you for being a role model," Sarah had written. "Thank you for giving me Nicole. I won the lottery in the second mom department."

For some reason that only Jacquie understood

completely, she had cornered Sarah in the kitchen that night and told her as much of her life story as she could in thirty minutes. Some of it Sarah had heard a hundred times before, but on that night, Mom wanted Sarah to know who she was, who she'd been. Sarah and I giggled about it that night, but now accept it as a magical gift.

My mom always showed up for Sarah and her brother, Tony, even though they weren't her biological grandchildren. She didn't miss their graduations; never missed a school play or a birthday celebration. She knew all their friends. Her loss had been especially hard on Sarah.

That Thanksgiving before she died, she had somehow been more Jacquie than ever. She always brought her unique craziness, and she knew it, and we all used to laugh, but this last year she'd been even more quirky than usual. At one point during our Thanksgiving celebration she'd said, "Is that a new dog?"

"No, Mom," I said, "that's Diesel. I've had Diesel for three and a half years."

"I've never seen that dog in my life," she said.

The next day, I later learned, Mom had called one of her best friends, Tina, and said, "Can you believe Nicole tried to convince me that dog wasn't new?"

When we sat down at the table for Thanksgiving

dinner, we were sitting once again at a table we'd had for seven years. My mom loved that table, but she hated the chairs; they were too low and heavy. And every year I'd say, "Well, it's my house. I like them. So I'm going to pull out the chair for you every year and I'm going to give you pillows."

This year, same as ever—but my mother said, "I don't need a pillow!"

Then, five minutes later, we go to sit down for dinner . . . and: "These chairs are so low—and I need a pillow!"

I had no idea what was going on; I shot Sarah a look, and we just laughed. She was so Jacquie that night . . .

(When I hugged her goodbye at the end of that meal, that was it—I couldn't have known, but that was the last time I would ever touch my mother, ever see her . . .)

In fact, that whole last year she was so *on purpose*—again, almost as if she knew something. Every Mother's Day she'd give me flowers, except this year she gave me a statue of Buddha with crystals glued onto it.

"I don't know," she said, "there was something about this. I said, 'Nicole has to have this.'"

Unlike flowers, it wasn't something I could ever throw away. I think of Mom every time I look at that statue that sits in my bathroom right next to my tub.

Laura 3:52

All these things were running through my grieving heart as I wandered through the house that early morning. Suddenly, as I turned around in the living room, there she was! I stood stock-still, moved and comforted by my mother's presence. Then she hugged me!

I checked my watch. It was 3:52 a.m. *You're waking up Laura at 3:33, and I get 3:52?*

Nothing made sense.

When I got the death certificate, the first thing I noticed was the time of death: 3:52 a.m.

One of my best friends since childhood, Anthony, came over a few nights into my grief. He had tried to time it so that we could be alone together, because he'd known my mom almost as long as I had.

When he arrived at the house, I greeted him with a long hug and some tears. Gathering myself back to the moment, I said, "Oh, my friend Laura is here; I hope you don't mind." If he was disappointed, he didn't let me know.

Anthony's father is an eminent director, so he'd grown up, like me, surrounded by famous people. He's unimpressed by fame, but that night, he urgently pulled me to one side.

"You know when you said 'Laura' earlier? Well, idiot, you forgot the Dern! Oh my God . . . just, oh my God!" It was fun to see him speechless and starstruck for once. Laura has that effect on people.

To me, though, she was simply my friend, always exactly what the people around her needed. She had driven from funeral home to funeral home for me, trying to find the best place for my mother to rest.

I was surrounded by love; it had helped keep my mother close and it had brought her to me at 3:52. And every minute since.

SEVEN

How to Be Sorry

Jacquie Avant was always the epitome
of kindness. Of grace. Just such a good
and decent person. I know I hadn't
seen her in years, but she has left
a lasting impact on me.

What do I want my heart to be like? Hatred should not
be the shape of my heart, nor should vengefulness. As
it says in 1 John 3:18: "My little children, let us not love in
word or in tongue, but in deed and in truth."

So do I want to get sick over the person who turned my
family's life upside down? What does it feel like to know
that this was the kind of human being my mother spent her
entire life trying to help?

The spiritual tools my mother gave me bring me back to center whenever I find myself veering off into hatred. Her lived example is like those bumpers in a bowling alley that keep little kids (and some of us adults!) from hurling their ball into the gutters.

Whenever I start to get angry, I think about what Mom said to me about disconnection. She would often comment on the fact that the majority of us walk these days with our heads down, both metaphorically and literally. We carry shiny little dopamine generators all day long, checking our texts, updating our Instagram, looking at TikTok instead of each other. I'm not some Luddite. I know the benefits of the internet and the global connections it can foster; I understand very well that the internet has enabled businesses like the company my husband works for to bring wonderful art to so many people around the world. But it's also true that these small computers we carry with us at all times have uncoupled us from each other. Real intimacy between people has been replaced by what *feels* like intimacy online, but which is actually the opposite. It's easy to hide behind a keyboard and criticize or spread hate or fakery and worse.

My mother surely didn't understand the disconnect, and not because she was too old for a cell phone or a Gmail account. She simply couldn't understand why everyone was attacking everyone else over every little thing.

To her, that aggression spoke of a broken sense of shared reality. To her—and yes, to me—there was a sense that we had forgotten the human, forgotten to listen to the person in front of us. We're humans first, humans before anything and everything. Occasionally, like every other Gen Xer, I'd rail about "those Millennials" or "that younger generation," but my mom would clap back at me.

"No," she'd say, "it's not them. Maybe they didn't have parents or positive role models to help raise them right."

Growing up, I had no choice but to watch *To Sir with Love* and *Porgy and Bess* and *Guess Who's Coming to Dinner* when they aired on television—not to mention *60 Minutes* every Sunday night.

I always enjoyed those viewings (even on those occasions when I protested), but I'd claim *It's a Wonderful Life* as the best movie of all. I've loved that film ever since my mother made me watch it one Christmas Eve when I was quite young. My brother and I would have preferred *The Sonny and Cher Show*, but my mother never missed a chance to educate us in what she felt really mattered. My young mind was captivated by the tribulations of George Bailey and the efforts of his guardian angel, Clarence. As the daughter of a man also called Clarence, who seemed to be an angel to many people who came through our house, I fell under the power of that movie, which has held me in its thrall ever since. George Bailey's angel was a bumbling old clockmaker with the surname of Odbody; the angel to many artists in Los Angeles back then was a foul-mouthed Black businessman. I guess you never get to know where your angel is coming from.

My father might have been an angel to my young imagination, but neither he nor my mother was my friend. They were my elders, my ancestors, my betters; they knew more than I, knew what I needed to know, and made sure I knew it.

In too many situations now, young people aren't being raised that way.

I was raised; *oh boy* was I raised. As my mom used to say, "It's called 'home training,' Nicole."

One time, I had been making T-shirts with my childhood friend Andrea; we were probably twelve years old. We'd been sticking beads on our shirts, painting them, all that, but eventually—while we were still engrossed—Andrea's mother arrived to pick her up. (And let me tell you, Andrea's mother came to our door, was invited in, and visited with my mother a little. That was crucial, and still should be—we really need to know where our children's friends are coming from, who their parents are. So many times kids are picked up from a playdate by parents who stay out in the car, so the parents never get acquainted.)

That day of the T-shirts, I had been so deep in the world of sequins and shiny baubles that I'd just said goodbye to Andrea and stayed with the amazing creations we'd been working on. (Wondrous though we thought they were, I'm sure we wore those T-shirts only once, if at all!)

But not accompanying Andrea to the door, not saying hello to her mother and goodbye to Andrea? File under: Really. Bad. Idea. My mother was horrified. As I was hot-gluing the last bead to my T-shirt, Mom stormed in, grabbed me by my ear, and dragged me toward the entryway.

"Get to that front door and say goodbye!" she hissed. "You have a guest. And she and her mom are leaving."

"Mom," I protested, "it's not that big of a deal."

Bad idea #2. Her grasp of my ear only got tighter, and I swear she put a little twist in it.

To my mother, as I should have known by then, this kind of thing defined "big deal."

Mom taught me to make my bed every day long before Admiral William H. McRaven famously told the graduating class at the University of Texas at Austin in 2014 the same thing. In fact, I still get chills of shame when I remember a day from my horrific preteens that I didn't make my bed and, when challenged on it, said, "We have a housekeeper. *She* can make my bed." (No, I really said that. I'm not proud.)

My mother looked at me, paused, took her glasses off—oh no, when she takes her glasses off, you know what's coming—and said, very calmly, "The housekeeper works for *me*. Make your bed."

This would pay off later at sleepaway camp, where I was the only kid who regularly and without prompting made her bed every day. "Nicole is the most lovely, polite, beautiful child. She doesn't fight back, she doesn't argue—and she always makes her bed!" my camp counselor wrote of me. I had taken my contrition at being thoughtless about the housekeeper and used it as fuel to improve my character.

My dad, unlike my mom, never took his glasses off when he was pissed; instead, he'd lower them to the end of his nose so that he could peer imperiously over them. Once, when I was working for him as a VP at his publishing company, I made the terrible mistake of criticizing one of his employees because she couldn't find a file or some such and hadn't called me back about it. To me, this was a sign of something, God knows what, and I'd pointed out her error to my father.

Bad idea #3. Dad just slipped his glasses low along his nose, looked at me, and said, "Come here."

You bet your hide I went.

"Okay," he said, so quietly it was almost hard to hear him. "Two things. One, you are totally in error." (This was a

Clarence-ism, and whenever he said it, you knew better than to question whether or not you were in error. You *were* in error; there was no court of appeal; and you were expected to be sorry about it.)

"More important," he went on, "let me ask you a question." When my father wanted to "ask you a question," that's when you knew he was *really* mad.

"Let me ask you a question," he repeated, in case I'd missed that he was steaming. (I hadn't.)

"Have *you* ever made a mistake?" he said.

What does one say to that? I said, "Yes . . ."

"Then how dare you? Who are you? That woman you're being so critical of? She's an elder. Get out of my office," he said.

On the drive home that day, I felt terribly small, as I should have. I knew I had to make amends, make a real apology, not just to my father, but to the woman I'd failed, too.

But even back then, I knew this much: forgiveness is a choice and a gift to yourself. Without it, your life is mired in poison.

+ + +

Susan Sarandos was a stay-at-home mom; she raised five kids in a lower-middle-class economic situation in Phoenix,

Arizona. (However, she made sure that there was a VCR in the house, which is incredible given what her fourth child, Theodore Anthony Sarandos Jr., co–chief executive officer and chief content officer for Netflix, ended up doing for a living.)

Forgiveness is a choice and a gift to yourself.

Ted once described his childhood this way: "I never felt like there was that much to lose. My background is very, very humble. It wasn't like my Ivy League education was on the line if I made a left instead of a right. I didn't have inspirational leaders to follow . . . I didn't have anyone to disappoint, so the things I was doing were out of passion and a desire to do better."

No one can unscramble an egg; you have to live with your past and overcome it, as Ted did. Ted had to find his own path. He doesn't lay blame at his parents' door for anything either; he just got on with it.

During the time I was living in the Bahamas and working as the US ambassador there, Ted was going through something pretty terrible: Susan got very sick. In those last weeks and months, Ted's entire family gathered around his mom to help. She was still in Arizona, and we went back and forth a fair bit, trying to care for her, but it was hard on everyone.

One day, one of his sisters called Ted and told him that Susan wasn't doing well, so again he flew to Arizona. A day or two later, during a session in which he was sitting with his mother, Ted went downstairs for a moment, and by the time he went back upstairs, his mother had passed. No one had expected Susan to die so suddenly. It was a truly tragic day.

(His pain was compounded in November 2021, when he lost his father, Ted Sr., just twelve days before my mother was killed. Ted Sr. was the kindest soul imaginable, and his loss was almost unbearable for Ted. My mom was killed on a Wednesday morning, and that following Saturday we had been due to bury Ted Sr.—so we were already in a state of deep grief when the unimaginable happened. I couldn't even be with Ted for his own father's funeral; so much is lost in these moments.)

Ted had been devastated by the loss of his mother, too. It didn't help that his wife was an ambassador more than two thousand miles away on an island in the Atlantic. The evening Susan died, I was in the back of my official car, and Ruben, my driver, and Joe, one of my night security guys, were up front. I spent a lot of time with those guys, and we'd all gotten to know each other pretty well. My phone lit up, and it was Ted, telling me his terrible news.

I was heartsick for him and told him how sorry I was—and also how sorry I was that I was stuck in the Bahamas.

Ready for my biggest mistake?

"When's the funeral?" I asked.

Ted, in his fresh grief, said, "Oh, I don't know yet. I mean, I have no idea . . ." and trailed off.

So I took the chance to dig a big fat hole of pain: "I hope it's not next Sunday," I said, "because I have a delegation coming from Washington. It's very important that this doesn't screw up my delegation. It's a big deal—we've been working for months to get them to show up, and . . ."

I'm sure I went on a bit further because I was in ambassador mode, not loving wife mode. But you get the terrible gist. Eventually I concluded, "Okay. Well, whatever. We'll figure it out."

With that, I hung up, noticing that we were almost back at the residence. Joe, my beloved security guy, turned to look at me from the front seat. If looks could cut, I would have bled. Ruben gave Joe the merest glance, too, but it was like ice in that car; and let me tell you, Ruben is the sweetest man who ever walked this planet. Me? Still pretty much oblivious—I had calls to make, and I had that delegation coming, and on and on and on.

When we reached the residence, Joe opened my door as usual, walked me up to the house, opened it up, checked all around inside to make sure it was safe, then okayed me in. I said, "Good night, Joe," and I got that same stiletto look as he murmured, "Good night, ma'am."

I remember thinking, on my way upstairs, "What is going *on* with everybody?" As I was getting ready for bed, I looked at myself in the mirror, and it hit me like a thunderbolt.

"Oh my God." I said it out loud. And then I looked at myself again—*really* looked at myself.

"I don't even know who you are," I told my reflection. "Where did you go? I don't even know. Who did you become?"

It was a terrible feeling: the realization that I'd become *that woman*, the one I always complained about—the woman who doesn't get it, the woman who can't understand, the woman who forgets about her family, who forgets about her children, who forgets about everything but herself. Who is worse than the worst man could ever be.

I knew what I had to do. With tears streaming down my face, I called Ted. "I swear to God," I said, sobbing, "you can divorce me tomorrow and you have every right to. I would completely understand. I'm so sorry."

◆ ◆ ◆

By that point in my life, I knew what forgiveness was.

Even before my terrible reaction to Ted's loss—but some

years after my earlier poor reaction to my colleague in Dad's office—I had been thinking about the magic of forgiveness; the magic of self-worth (if you can't forgive yourself, good luck forgiving anyone around you); the magic of trusting the Divine, of whom Micah says, "He does not retain His anger forever, because He delights in mercy" (7:18); the magic of your words and taking care in what you say—and how *all* these elements can all come together to create what I call "the magic of personal responsibility." This was the lesson my mother was teaching me by taking me to the Special Olympics, or by grabbing me by the ear when I was rude to a friend, or by telling me the simplest thing: make your damn bed. Same with my father—he was determined that I would understand the wisdom of my elders, be it Bill Withers or that colleague to whom I had been so rude.

Forgiveness is not condonement: we're not asked simply to overlook poor behavior. I didn't need Ted to condone my heartlessness; I needed him to forgive it. Forgiveness doesn't necessarily mean reconciliation either (though in the case of Ted, I was certainly hoping that would be where it led!). When you forgive, your job is simply to bless that person who has hurt you and give up your anger toward them. When you don't condone but forgive, you're more likely to be able to give up the negativity that comes with resentment, which means you don't harm yourself further.

Let's say someone close to you has truly hurt you with their behavior, and you never want to speak to them again. Fine: don't speak to them again if you don't have to!

Now, of course, I'm charged with the most difficult effort of forgiveness imaginable—forgiving the man who ended the wonderful life of my mother. Part of my forgiveness goes like this:

Mom's life hasn't ended—not really. She doesn't inhabit the past tense; she was *so* alive, filled the dash between birth and death dates with so many vibrant things, that the mere act of her murder cannot begin to end her presence in our lives.

But even that great positive, those thousands upon thousands of tiny moments with which she so gracefully filled the dash, even *that* cannot hold back my sense of desolation sometimes.

When Amy did that heroic thing of going to the house to retrieve important items, one of the objects she found was a bottle of holy water my mother had gotten from the River Jordan some decades earlier. Mom had kept it in its little plastic bottle all those years. Amy said she found it behind a picture of me and my mom that stood in my mother's office. I've since placed it on the tray next to my bed, the one that holds my perfumes, trinkets, rings, bookmarks, glasses . . .

One evening, I'd been sitting with my father in the garden when, out of nowhere, he lowered his head in despair. "When is Jacqueline coming back?" he said, quietly. "She just . . . disappeared."

The world stopped. What does one say to a ninety-something man when he asks a question like that? I'm a problem-solver—nothing makes me happier—but there's no problem-solving this particular situation.

"She's not coming back, Dad," I said, as kindly as I could. "I'm really sorry. Hopefully you'll see her again."

That night, I found myself sitting on the end of our bed, completely furious and defeated. My father described my mother, his wife, as "disappeared," regularly and to everyone. He may have said "killed" once or twice, but mostly "disappeared" was the word he used. The poignancy of that wrecked me; I found myself screaming and wailing.

"What the hell is going on?" I yelled at Ted. "What am I supposed to tell my father? No one has an answer for me. What am I supposed to say to this man?"

What had happened to us wasn't some kind of magic trick, nor had Mom been struck by lightning. But there was no googling "What do you say to a man whose wife has been senselessly murdered after decades of marriage?"

Ted knew, it seemed, that there was nothing to be said in the face of my storm. These were just the moments that we had to walk through together and alone.

Ted also knows I'm a thrower, so when I picked up the

bedside tray covered in perfumes, trinkets, and holy water, he quickly said, "Don't do it—the holy water! Don't fuck up the holy water!"

But it was too late—I hurled that tray with all the grief and frustration and sense of injustice my body could manage. What had happened to my mother had been so . . . reckless, had so revealed the lack of value that had been placed upon her life. I was furious that this type of evil energy, an energy that roams the earth all too often, had been visited upon my parents' legendary and kind home. And I hadn't been able to save her from it, couldn't now save my father.

The crash of that tray could be heard all over Los Angeles, I imagine. There was a hole in the wall, perfume everywhere . . . then silence.

The holy water, being in a plastic bottle, survived, but my anger didn't. I sat back down at the mirror of my vanity and cried.

"I don't know what to tell him," I wailed to Ted, who came to wrap me in his arms. "What just happened to my life? I know things change; nothing is guaranteed; you really don't know what's ahead until change actually comes. But my world is completely upside down. I feel like the house landed on me as it did on a witch in *The Wizard of Oz* and I'm just trying to push it off me. I don't know how to do this." And with that, I proceeded to cry it out until my eyes were swollen.

◆ ◆ ◆

One day in June 2020, Ted came to find me in our house. What he told me devastated me; I howled like a wounded animal.

I had been friends with Steve for most of my life. He and I shared a connection that ran very deep, to our souls. We'd known each other as young kids on the west side of Los Angeles—our moms were both very involved in philanthropic work, and we were often the kids in the corner rolling our eyes at what we perceived as boring events. Later, as we grew up, we'd both turn to philanthropy ourselves, and we loved talking about it, and about politics and music and how we could best serve others and make a true and positive impact on other people's lives.

It was Steve who was always pushing me to show up more for others, for the underdog. Steve saw, really *saw*, everyone—the waiter, the janitor, the gas station attendant, the bus driver, the teacher . . . *everyone*. He didn't care about what was in their bank account or what people could do for him. He cared about people themselves, cared about their souls and their hearts. He instinctively knew that he was no better than anyone else and that they were no less than he.

When the pandemic arrived, Steve made it his business to check in on me regularly. He'd often ask to come over, or suggest that I visit him. But like so many of us, I was being hypervigilant about the virus, especially with elderly parents. I would say, "Yes, of course, soon. Let's wait, though, and see about this damn COVID."

In the meantime, Steve took to driving all over Los Angeles County, searching for restaurants and diners that were still open, anyone who was serving takeout. He'd buy a meal, drive somewhere up into the canyons, then sit on the roof of his car and marvel at the stunning views of our gorgeous city and county.

He'd sometimes ask me to join him. "Tomorrow, my friend," I'd say. "I'll call you tomorrow and we'll make a plan!"

Then, one day in June, Ted found me in the house, told me the terrible news, and I realized that I would never have another tomorrow with Steve. My heart felt physically ripped out of my body. Steve had died that afternoon in a tragic and violent way.

Steve had been battling depression for years, but he made sure to *never* take me or anyone else down his path into hell with him. Instead, he'd simply tried to connect with me. Could I have helped him see around the bend into a more hopeful future? I'll never know. Instead, I'd shown up in the way that had been most comfortable for *me*, not the way he needed. He had simply wanted to see me, to talk, to connect; and I failed him.

It took almost two years for me to finally get to a place of forgiving myself by casting this burden of guilt and shame upon the Lord. In those two years, I had to do a deep dive into my own behavior; I had to be accountable for it, and then finally offer my sorrow to Steve's beautiful soul and leave it at the altar.

It was a very difficult journey. But I know now that the lesson showed up just in time. By the time I received that last text from my mom, I had truly started to learn and live the lesson that tomorrow is never promised, ever. It's not promised to any of us, so we must always take that extra step to respond to those closest to us. In the words of Matthew 25:13: "Watch therefore, for you know neither the day nor the hour . . ."

I never wanted to feel again that pain and guilt of not showing up or responding to someone, because not responding *is* a response. My mom deserved a response and her favorite emoji before I took a bath that fateful December night, so that's what I sent her. Simple, but everything—a lesson from my friend Steve, and one I live by, every day now, and always will.

◆ ◆ ◆

When I found out that someone had shot my mom, one of my first thoughts was "Oh God, please don't let me hate this man. Give me the strength to not hate him."

In fact, I didn't want to even think about him. I would pray that he was put in jail for the rest of his life so that he couldn't harm anybody else, but hate was another thing entirely, and I wanted no part of it. I told myself, "I forgive his soul. I do not condone the act, but I forgive his soul." I knew that if I harbored any hate or animosity toward him, it would make me sick and depressed.

Alternatively, even now, I think instead of someone like the police officer who rode with my mother, and who took me to one side at the hospital. "I want to tell you something," he said. "I was riding in the back of the ambulance with your mom. She's a really strong woman. She was *living*. She was *breathing*. I've seen twenty-year-olds get shot like that, and they're done. Not your mom—and at eighty-one . . . ?" His voice trailed off; he seemed to be reliving the trauma of it.

Not responding *is* a response.

(Of course, my mother *would* get the best-looking cop in the world. He looked like Daniel Truhitte, who played the telegraph boy, Rolfe, in *The Sound of Music*.)

Despite all this trauma, I believe in redemption, but I also believe in accountability and consequences for one's behavior. What really matters is that I give him zero power over me and my family.

It's all too easy to fall into the blame game, and there's no upside to that. In my own life, I try to keep negative people out. I bless them with love, but life is short and precious, and I want to live in a space filled with good energy. No one gets to come into your "country" and put you down; no one gets to belittle you; and for sure, no one gets to own your heart. And if someone *does* wrong you, you need to forgive and move on. Forgiveness is a kind of surrender: it's giving up the anger, the disappointment, the betrayal. But as I noted earlier, it never means condoning the act or forcing reconciliation. It's nice when reconciliation happens, but I've learned that it isn't necessary at all. In fact, "Bye, friend" with a smile is sometimes necessary! Forgiveness won't always be easy, but when we think of what others have done to lead us all into the light, we should be grateful, and we should use our gratitude to establish who we are and what we're willing to take.

One thing I know: I'm sadly not alone in having to forgive and to be forgiven.

Ted forgave me for my thoughtlessness about the loss of his mother; I didn't deserve it, but he forgave me anyway—that's what love is, that's what *his* love is. Love is being able to be the very worst version of yourself and still know that the person who loves you will continue to love you. (It goes both ways, of course: love is also being able to continue to love the very worst version of your partner.) Love isn't about romance, or roses, or rowing out on a clear-blue lake to an island, where the sweetest of breezes gently rustle the palm trees. Love is about hearing your wife, over two thousand miles away, really not get it *at all*—and at such a crucial and sensitive time—and *still* forgiving her, quickly and completely.

To complete the process of forgiveness, you have one additional task: give up your anger and bless the person who wronged you—in other words, genuinely wish him or her the very best. Say, "I bless you with love, and I release you in peace," over and over. No, I mean it—you have to say it out loud, though no one has to hear it but you! I've had to do this many times in my life. It dissipates the anger and releases the magic of gratitude and the magic of forgiveness.

Alternatively, you can write an angry letter to the person who hurt you; but you don't send it, you burn it. I've done that so many times that if anyone smells smoke in my house, the joke is, "Oh my God, who's Nicole forgiving now?"

+ + +

About a week after that terrible phone call with Ted—the call that I took while in the Bahamas—I said to Joe, "I got your look, you know—not in that moment, but later."

Joe laughed and said, "I gave you that look because I wanted you to just maybe question yourself."

And it worked. Joe had given me an incredible gift, one that I didn't deserve (which made it all the sweeter).

I'll never forget the love those people in the Bahamas showed me, and the forgiveness they showered me with. They didn't condone my mistakes, but they forgave me for my failings.

THE GRASS BENEATH MY FEET

Especially in the first weeks after my mother's death, people would ask me how I could even get out of bed. It wasn't easy—that's for sure. Even now, it sometimes takes some doing.

Here's my two-part recipe: Every evening I have a bath and meditate, say the Lord's Prayer, and then run through all the things I'm grateful for. Then, in the morning, I read out loud my affirmations while I sip on some tea—this sets the tone for my day. And I ask for those blessings of the Divine that I mentioned earlier.

But the morning of December 1, 2021, was different. On that first morning after Mom's death, after I'd gotten back home from the hospital, Gwyneth took me to one side.

"You're not even in your body right now," she said. "I need you to look at me. Do you understand what happened?"

I hesitated. "Yeah . . . ?" I said, looking somewhere into the middle distance.

"No," she said, "*look* at me. Do you understand what happened? Somebody broke into your mom's house. Somebody shot her. Your mom was murdered."

The middle distance still held what attention I could muster. The silence between us was like a dense mist. "Let's go walk outside," she suggested.

Outside in my garden, we took our shoes off and just walked.

"We have to get you grounded," Gwyneth said. "You need to walk on the grass because you're not grounded. It's okay that you're not." So we walked, and I felt the reality of the earth, still spinning, still growing and dying and growing again.

Later, Candace joined us at the kitchen table. "Go take a shower," Candace said. "Go to sleep. Go scream. Go kick or cry. You do whatever you want. Just know that you don't have to do anything to take care of anybody. We're here."

Their support was especially beautiful because they knew that service was one of my "love languages," but they also knew that it wasn't the language I should be speaking right then.

I was like a newborn, learning to breathe and live and eat and feel anew.

Was I now going to be identified, whenever I walked into a party or a store or a meeting, as "the woman whose mom was murdered"? Was that to be my identity now?

In the worst moments, the best people find a way to

give you exactly what you need. I was learning this every single day. I didn't really want anyone to tell me what had happened to my mom, but what my friends did was exactly what was needed at exactly the right moment.

I had felt the grass between my toes and had exhaled, even if for a moment only.

It was enough.

EIGHT

No Comfort Zones

Always elegant. Always that smile. Always
that little twinkle. A beauty for the ages.

So many of us have had it relatively easy. But that doesn't
mean we get to coast, as we've been doing for so long.
We have to get involved and make our elders proud of us; we
have to mourn those we've lost and start to care for those
who are left. And we can do that only by letting the magic
of the Divine lead us and heal us, as it's led and healed the
sorrowful for all these years (and will again).

Because I grew up in a house that had a revolving door
of famous names coming to parties, to meetings, to see my
father and mother, I was able to witness how Clarence and
Jacqueline brought everyone together to make great music,

great movies, and better politics. As I matured, I saw that "getting involved" is not just for professional politicians; it's for all of us, and we're all called to do it. The magic of getting involved creates a sense of community, of common purpose, and of leaving aside one's personal needs for the greater good.

Accordingly, I didn't know any different; getting involved was just what you did.

It's what many, many people do. Despite all the terrible things that happened during COVID, if you looked hard enough, you could see innumerable moments of wonderful involvement and commitment, too. First responders and caregivers all over the United States and around the world committed themselves every day, every shift, to love their patients above all else. Those heroes in many cases left behind their own families. There was, for example, the doctor in Spain who didn't hug his children for a month; he was on twenty-four-hour rotating cycles, and on his limited hours off he kept himself apart to safeguard his family's health. There were the forty-three workers at a Braskem America factory in Delaware who didn't go home for twenty-eight days in order to reduce the risk of COVID (and thus the risk of factory slowdowns) while they produced millions of pounds of material needed to make personal protective equipment. There were millions of nurses and janitors and orderlies, grocery store staff and bus drivers, and frontline workers who never once shirked their commitment to healing. I've been thinking a lot about how each of these wonderful people chose love, when it would have been understandable if they'd wanted to hide at home like the rest of us. They didn't do so, however; they showed up—they saw the need, and they got involved, and they resisted their fear, and they loved.

That's really all they did: they loved. But that is everything. When challenges face us down, we have to turn to love; we have to be loving, because the opposite only causes more heartache. This is the magic that will save us, in a pandemic, when we lose someone close, or in the future when new bad—and good!—things happen. The magic of love.

＋ ＋ ＋

In the Bahamas, we at the US Embassy made a huge deal of the Special Olympics organization. We even had two of founder Eunice Shriver's granddaughters, Eunice and Francesca, come to visit—that, in turn, got the then Bahamian prime minister Hubert Ingraham to join us, which was wonderful and a surprise (great prime minister, just not much of a people person).

Beyond the Shrivers, we brought in basketball legend

Magic Johnson; Andrew Sharpless, the CEO of the conservation group Oceana; and activist and educator Geoffrey Canada.

Magic Johnson was an amazing catalyst for action during my time in the Bahamas. His visit catapulted us to the next level; it proved that we could show off the very best of the United States and inspire people to action. His sharing of his story opened countless doors for me as ambassador; and it illustrated once again the power of connections and face time with incredible people. Magic's visit uplifted the view of the US Embassy in those islands—it was clear that we could get things done.

+ + +

One of the most memorable visits to the Bahamas during my ambassadorship was from Holly Robinson Peete and her husband, former NFL quarterback Rodney Peete. My staff and I had planned an autism awareness event, and the State Department had sent me talking points for it. Though the prep documents were solid and true, there was no heart in their words. A story works only if it's authentic, which is why I asked Holly and Rodney to come to the Bahamas to speak. (Their son Rodney Jr. has autism.) Holly was incredible, and the power of her talk was further deepened by Rodney's testimony. He gave a speech to all those stuffy and important Bahamian men in which he cried.

"I know what it feels like to have your son bounce a basketball all day and he can't stop," Rodney said. "I know what it's like to have a son who's banging his head against the wall for six hours and you can't stop him. I know what it feels like to go to the doctor and have the doctor tell you, 'Your child may never tell you that he loves you.'" Doctors, the most prominent Bahamian businessmen, the entire front row—*all* of them were crying.

Then there would be times where during my ambassadorship I, too, would be crying.

◆ ◆ ◆

If you decide you want to find a yellow Volkswagen when you're out driving today, I can guarantee that's what you'll find. If you want to find problems, you can find them; but it's the same with positives, too. One day I was complaining about something, and my friend Penny said, "Well, what did you expect? You're focused entirely on what's wrong. Why don't you tell me what's right instead? Did you have any food today? Do you have fancy dinner plans? Are you taking a bus or a car? Do you have gas in the car?"

"Oh," I said, "are we going down *that* rabbit hole?"

"Yes," she said, "we *are* going down that rabbit hole, because I'm going to teach you how to switch gears and shut the f--- up."

I seem to have a penchant for attracting people who keep me honest. My friend Amanda always makes me get to the point, makes me drill down into what's going on in my heart. Every time I call her in a spiral, she cuts me off: "What do you *really* want?" she says. "I have five minutes. I have to take the girls to school, so what is it that you want? What's your *intention?*"

And then there's my mother. She wasn't the most patient person, even with me. Sometimes I'd call her to talk about something, and if I started to wander, she'd say, "Are you finished?" or "Is there anything else?"

Or, the best of all, she'd cut me off with a simple "Anyway . . ."

"Mom!" I'd say, "that's so rude. Show some patience!"

That was Mom: she wouldn't deal with anybody's shit. She was a real New Yorker. (Later, I was able to tell her that sometimes that approach to interpersonal relationships can make people feel a bit . . . *unimportant*, and she said, "Hmm—that wasn't kind of me, not mature. I apologize.")

As for Penny's influence on me, it spread out into the rest of my life. Adapting her message, I started telling my kids that they were too focused on the rearview mirror.

We were out driving one day, and one of the kids was complaining about something that had happened. "Why do you think the rearview mirror is so small?" I asked, glancing at them in its little rectangle. Without waiting for them to answer, I kept going: "I'll tell you. It's teeny because you're supposed to look in your past just to grab a lesson. Grab the lesson and then move on. In every adversity there are two positive outcomes: the lesson and the blessing."

They didn't look convinced, so I tried again. "You look in the past, grab the lesson, and move forward," I said. "But your future is right here. Your future is all in front of you. And it's huge and immediate."

But perspective is everything; I was to learn that in the Bahamas.

✦ ✦ ✦

Look to the past to grab the lesson, then move forward.

No one ever grew and matured by keeping still in the status quo; and no one ever changed anything without first telling a story. Stories are the most powerful way to make change. The magic of someone opening up and revealing themselves never fails to inspire a new way of looking at the world.

One of the most meaningful and powerful things I got to do in the Bahamas was to get involved with young people at two detention centers on the islands. I had grown very interested in the girls' center in particular—the Willie Mae Pratt Centre for Girls. There was just something about those girls that moved me greatly; I found myself heading there every couple of weeks.

What I remember most about those girls was the look in their eyes. You could tell that they just wanted someone to see them and see past their bad behavior, see past the mistake that had landed them in a correctional facility. As a Black woman in the United States, I was used to not being seen, and I was determined to show these girls that they were seen and heard—and not for what they'd done wrong, but for what they could do right in the future.

Again, this wasn't about condoning what they'd done—it was about letting their future be more important than their past. And *they* didn't seem to condone their wrongs either. I didn't sense that they were trying to find someone else to blame; most of them had accepted their punishment as a first step in creating a more meaningful life.

Bill Withers once said of my father, "He puts people together, and they do what they do." And that's what I felt was happening for me at Willie Mae Pratt: I wanted to put people together and let them do what they do so that the lesson in adversity could also be the blessing.

As my involvement at the center was deepening, we were planning a women's empowerment day, and I asked Shaun Robinson, from *Access Hollywood*, to come to the Bahamas—specifically, to Willie Mae Pratt. She graciously agreed. While she was there, she took the time to talk to the girls about her book, *Exactly as I Am*, for which she'd interviewed lots of celebrities—Sharon Stone, Arianna Huffington, India.Arie, and others—all in order to help young women understand how to live better lives. It was a wonderful day, completely opening the floodgates for the girls to tell their stories, to be finally seen as people who'd made mistakes, not as problems no one could fix.

One story from the book, in particular, and one girl at Willie Mae Pratt who read that story, really resonated with me. This girl specifically picked out India.Arie's story—she said it made her "heart break open." When I asked her why, she said, "Because I've always felt ugly. People used to tease me at school and say I was ugly. I had bad skin. I didn't feel pretty, and I was teased. I've always felt so lonely."

When I got back to the embassy—and me being me—I called my friend Ron, who I knew was managing India .Arie. I told him I was having a Fourth of July party, and we needed to get India.Arie to it. I figured it might be a long shot, but I didn't account for her generosity. Not only did she attend, but she graciously agreed to play a show. And then I stole her away to go with me to Willie Mae Pratt.

Imagine the scene when India.Arie walked into that facility. That one young girl who had picked out her story started crying hysterically; India was like a dream to her.

India said, "I thank you so much for loving my story." Then, to the girls' delight, she stayed to sing songs and sign autographs and take pictures. I can only think that India saved some lives that day.

✦ ✦ ✦

India's efforts were matched by those of a very different person.

Admiral James Alexander "Sandy" Winnefeld Jr.—the vice chairman of the Joint Chiefs of Staff from 2011 to 2015—came to the Bahamas and really wanted to go to the boys' equivalent of Willie Mae Pratt, the Simpson Penn Centre for Boys. He wanted to hear the boys' stories, and he wanted to share his own (including juicy facts like that his great-grandfather had been a Prussian cavalryman, and that Winnefeld Jr. himself had worked as a consultant on the movie *Top Gun*!). He wanted to share his story so that these boys could see what it would take to rise above their situations and make something beautiful of their lives.

But first? He shot baskets with the kids (in his admiral's uniform, no less!); and then, when he'd gained their respect, the boys in turn were open to hearing him out about discipline and commitment and turning their lives around. (I'm not sure he would have gotten through to them in the same way if he hadn't had a perfectly presentable jump shot.)

Forget preaching a sermon; you have to *be* the sermon. As Matthew 7:16 tells us: "You will know them by their fruits."

That's what Winnefeld taught those boys that day, and what India showed those girls. Just saying something isn't enough; you have to stand for something, so that even before you open your mouth, people will know what you believe in.

You have to show up and share your story.

+ + +

I don't claim that any of the sacrifices I've made have come close to the ones made by my forebears; but I, too, understand what sacrifice means, and how its blessings can make a radical difference to individual lives and to the life of a nation.

In the aftermath of letting Ted down during that phone call after his mom's death, I realized something very important: my responsibility to him and our family was just as important as the job that I was doing in the Bahamas.

This left me with a monumentally hard decision. I'd finally cracked the job of ambassador, and now I might have to give it up? I wasn't sure that my marriage could survive a longer stint of us being apart, and yet I couldn't serve as ambassador without living in the Bahamas. Ted was very busy with his job—I got that—but so was I. Why did I have to quit *mine*? Why was it up to *me* to make that sacrifice? I'd finally gotten comfortable in my gig and settled in on the islands. I'd made friends, I had my rhythm with them, and the job was really rewarding—and now I had to make a decision: Do I want this enough to keep my energy and focus here, or do I shift focus to my family, who needs me—a family I might not have in six months or eight months if I continue as ambassador? In the end, I submitted my letter of resignation.

I'll be honest: I was angry that I had to make that decision.

Giving up the ambassadorship, with all its challenges and rewards, wasn't the end of this issue, of course. I still had to work out how to be a powerful woman married to a powerful man, and weigh what that asked of me as a supporter of him. I think a lot of women face this issue: as much as they want to be a badass in their own career, they also have a calling to serve and care; it's in a woman's very DNA to nurture.

So how to square that circle? I don't pretend to have answers—it's an age-old conundrum, and we women have had few examples of high-powered partnerships to learn from—but I will say this: I think the answer revolves around radical self-care. Being a leader while supporting a leader means we have to reinvent the role of women in the workplace—hell, we have to write a whole new guidebook!—and it has to center on taking real time for ourselves, committing to affirmations and prayer and time to rejuvenate and heal. We need to commit to meaningful self-management, because if we don't manage ourselves—physically, emotionally, spiritually—we'll find ourselves running on empty, and that will stop us being able to properly serve those around us. (You have to fill your own tank; yes, you have to serve yourself as well as others.)

I've found for myself that healing and self-care come via *doing*—being active, always keeping myself in motion. My survival, and the survival of my father after the loss of his wife and my mother, happened only because I took a leaf out of her playbook and committed to being at all times involved. This is how I'm guiding us into a new destiny. The world told me I should crater in my trauma; instead, I invited friends in to help, and I kept active.

I'll say it again: sacrifice of any kind is never easy. And yet sacrifice is required in the decisions that so many women, especially, must face as we attempt to achieve a balance between work and the rest of life. It's the scourge of female competence: we already have to juggle many more things than men do, and we're the ones more likely to make sacrifices to ensure that everything holds.

But looked at another way, this was also a question of personal responsibility, because what's more important than family? I was failing my family because my job was so all-encompassing, despite Ted's remarkable support throughout my time in the Bahamas; and now Ted was also facing a massive uptick in what his job was asking of him. (Netflix was about to launch *House of Cards* back then, thereby inventing binge-watching!) Something had to give, and I felt it had to be me; I was the one who had to stretch to accommodate the changes that were needed.

There were many days I found myself shaking my fist at God, asking, "Why do we women have to be so darned *competent?*" But still, I was determined to forge a new way, to be a leader while supporting a leader. I'd done it with Obama, and I was doing it with Ted; I would come to do it later, too, with other politicians, and with my grieving father. For Ted's part, he was busy building a company, and I wanted to support that, but that didn't mean that I had to give up my own agency, my own sense of leadership. Yet the only way to make it all work was to do it with my whole heart.

This is the crucial thing: you should do something with every part of you, or not do it at all. As I like to tell our children, "Ain't no half-steppin' here!" Half measures never change anything; they lead only to resentment and bitterness. No, I didn't want to leave the Bahamas right then,

You should do something with every part of you, or not do it at all.

but I wanted my marriage to work and my family to be together. Once I understood that, the "sacrifice" turned into just how life was—an example of my father's mantra "It is what it is." Around that time, I wrote in my journal, "Put a bookmark in some of the more painful parts of your life; don't make that pain the book cover."

I just had to find out what my new role would be. What was I willing to sacrifice to move forward in life?

JOHN RICH

One of my more unlikely friendships is with musician John Rich. On the night my mother died, he tweeted, "I have friends from all walks of life, and Mr. Clarence Avant is one of them. He's one of the most influential people to ever be in music and he and Ms. Jacqueline have treated me like family for decades. Prayers up for the Avant family tonight."

The fact that John and I are friends is a miracle. Nothing about the two of us would have predicted our friendship.

John is a country musician, and a really good one. For a long time, he'd had the idea that he wanted to help heal the racial divide in America by bringing country music and Black music together. So he did the smart thing: he called my father for help. But we'd never heard of him in the office, so we just shrugged and moved right along.

Eventually we connected again, and he played at a fundraiser I was involved with in New York. After that, I would see John every so often, but most of the time we talked on the phone. We'd strategize about how to harness the American spirit. Whether you say, "We can do it!" like Rosie the Riveter in World War II, or "Yes we can," like the 2008 presidential campaign for Obama, the net result is the same. Americans will execute together like champs if we have a common goal.

But when I would talk excitedly about pushing the nation toward good, John would often stop me to ask if I was pushing *myself*. Was I pushing through my Beverly Hills bubble? Was I reaching up? And reaching down? Did I take the time to listen? Did I allow myself to be uncomfortable in the service of others? Was I brave?

He pushed me into unfamiliar spaces to fend for myself, and he kicked me out of my comfort zone every chance he could.

John helped me learn to find common ground with just about anyone, even if it was the tiniest sliver of turf. He helped me stay open to new people and possibilities. And we certainly don't agree on everything. But when I got the ambassadorship to the Bahamas, John called to say, "I'm bringing my guitar to the State Department. What song do you want me to play?"

◆ ◆ ◆

John Rich

On October 1, 2017, a man opened fire on over twenty-two thousand people at a music festival on the Las Vegas Strip. Perched in the window of a luxury hotel, he killed sixty people and left more than eight hundred injured. It was the worst mass shooting in modern American history.

John and his band had just finished performing when the massacre started. They had led the thousands of voices in singing "God Bless America" at the end of their set.

I had no idea if John was safe when I heard about the shooting. I just kept texting him, and pacing, and urging God, "I need to know that my friend is alive."

I prayed. I prayed. I prayed. I prayed for John. I prayed for the victims. I prayed for all the terrified souls in Vegas. I prayed for our nation to do something about these senseless murders. And yes, selfishly, I prayed for God to help me if something had happened to John Rich.

A text finally came. Right after his part of the gig, John had headed back to his Vegas honky-tonk, the Redneck Riviera. (I'd taken Ted to the opening of that place—I'm positive we were the only Democrats there—and Ted had said, "Only Nicole would bring us to this shit-kicking bar!") That terrible day in Vegas John had planned to throw a party for his beloved fans and friends there; they were all behind locked doors and out of harm's way when the shooting started.

When John was asked about what had happened that day in Vegas, he had a simple answer: "The devil showed up in the window of that hotel room."

One day recently my father was all at sea, lost, trying to come to terms with what had befallen us all. "What *happened*?" he asked plaintively.

"A devil showed up in the window," I said.

But here's something else: God was there, too. Just as God had saved John Rich and many others in Vegas that day, so God helped my mom by not urging her to run back to the bedroom or scream.

God filled my mother with his power that night. The devil energy will always try to show up; it's up to us to see that God is there, too, and to remember that we have free will to choose one way or the other.

NINE

Ask Not What Your Country

She was the rare adult who never looked
at you like you were just "some kid," but
rather had the ability to make you feel
like you were a person who was just as
important as one of the grownups.

It's time to shift our energies.

We are all responsible for our own energy. Bad things
happen, but they don't need to take away from your intention to do the right thing. Your energy is reflected in the
words you choose to speak—words that affect your behavior.
If you're negative all day long, how do you expect to have

a happy life? If the choice between a friendly or an un-friendly universe is in front of you, which one are you going to choose?

We are all our own radio towers, sending out various frequencies; but we're also like the radio itself—we can tune in to whatever we want. If you want to be negative, that's what you'll tune in to. If you want to think positively about life, then you can tune in to that frequency. It's just like improv comedy, where the rule is "Yes, and . . ." In light of that rule, if one comic says, "Oh, here comes a pink elephant!" the other comics don't say, "Nope, no elephant here"—they say, "Yes, and it's heading straight for us! Run!" (Or whatever—hopefully comics are funnier than that!)

That's how I'm trying to live now—giving off the right frequency, tuning in to the positive, and committing to "yes-and" thinking. Yes, I'm grieving, *and* I'm immensely grateful that my dad is living here with us. (Yet again he's found somewhere to lay his head, as he says; he always does.) Yes, I'm terribly sad that my mom is gone, *and* I'm grateful that she was such a powerful force in my life. This is not denial; Lord knows there are many days when I'm terribly sad. In fact, I grieve heavier some days than others, *and* I'm moving forward because I'm standing in my faith; I'm standing up tall because I'm standing in my faith. My mom would want me to move forward—not just want, *expect*.

I think I'm actually scared of her on the other side! There will be a reckoning, and that's no bad thing. I can't afford to squander the model she created for life. She was a powerful, get-shit-done person; she stood for things; she brought people together, made people's lives better—so who am I to be crushed by her loss to the point of squandering that template? It's more than being "not what she wanted." It's not who she was; it's not the daughter she raised, either.

I've changed since Mom died. For one thing, I have a real sense of urgency about everything—all must be done *now*. According to scripture, now is *always* the appointed time: "Now it is high time to awake out of sleep; for now our salvation is nearer than when we first believed" (Romans 13:11); and "Do you not say, 'There are still four months and then comes the harvest'? Behold, I say to you, lift up your eyes and look at the fields, for they are already white for harvest!" (John 4:35). So when folks call to speak to my father and he's napping, I wake him; after all, who knows how much time we have left with him?

Hand in hand with this renewed sense of urgency is a greater effort at planning and structure. I used to let things slide a little bit, as we all do sometimes, but not anymore. I'm acutely aware of the press of time, the fact that things can be taken away in an instant. Yes, I'm trying to be kind and patient with myself; yes, I'm choosing to believe things can only get better; yes, I let the chips fall where they may; yes, I am cultivating a grateful heart and a sound mind. But I'm doing it all today, this hour, this minute.

In short, I'm turning into Jacquie! Ted has said as much; he says, smiling, "Oh, she's in our house now."

◆ ◆ ◆

About five weeks after my mother died, I realized with a start that the birthday of one of my dearest friends was approaching. One evening, as I chatted to my mom as I took my bath, I found myself thanking her for making such a fuss about birthdays. Mom hated it if you tried to pass off the big day as no big deal. "You know for sure you're going to reach fifty?" she'd ask. "Every day people get on the freeway thinking they'll be home for dinner, but they aren't. Get with it—it's a birthday!"

I decided there and then that I was going to make a big deal of my friend Sara's birthday. She protested, assuming I wouldn't have the emotional space for it, but I told her about my mom's view on birthdays and explained that it would be the greatest gift to be able to celebrate in my home. I invited all our friends, got pizza and wine, and for the first time really since the terrible events of December, we got to be joyous; we got to laugh. This was probably the first significant moment in my healing process. The evening opened my heart in a new way. I thought, "This stuff is real; we have to celebrate *life!*" It helped that Sara is completely hilarious and brought her usual positive energy to the evening. It was wonderful to spend normal time with a funny person, away from having to relive everything.

In the face of death, sometimes you just need to live.

◆ ◆ ◆

My family has been faced with some stark choices. We could have gone negative, sullen, angry, vengeful, but we chose not to.

As I've said, imagination is the greatest tool humans have: we can picture *anything*! So why not try to always picture something really good? It doesn't matter if what you imagine is real or not—your subconscious doesn't know the difference, doesn't know if it's fake or real. Either way, focusing on the positive changes everything in your body. I know this as a truth since December 2021.

Sure, there have been days, weeks, even months since the murder of my mother when it's proven very hard to have a positive, forward-looking imagination. But I was lucky. Because of the power of my mother's example, and the lasting effects of her presence—seen so clearly in the things she was working toward, the organizations she supported, the fact that at eighty-one she was still urging herself forward relentlessly, tirelessly—I never entered into a spiral that I couldn't pull out of. I didn't find myself every day wondering, *Why my mother? Why my father? Why us?* Instead, grief felt like a boot camp. I would sit and think, "Okay, this is day two. This sucks. This is real. And we need to move forward while we're grieving. We need to move forward while we're angry."

I don't want this to sound as if I didn't sleep, didn't rest, didn't sit down. I did all those things, but I avoided the uselessness of what-ifs. I was determined to see exactly where I was and what was happening to and around me. I didn't have to imagine the worst thing; it had happened. I heard one story of someone after 9/11 who wouldn't return to work in Manhattan. When pressed as to why, she said that she was afraid something else really terrible would happen. But the worst *had* happened back then, and it had happened now to us. It was my job, my urgent focus, to acknowledge that this was where we were right then. The only thing that mattered then or matters now, the only thing any of us should be involved in, the only thing that is real and true and incontrovertible is the *present*.

In the face of death, sometimes you just need to live.

The truth—that's all there is. It doesn't matter if I wish

something weren't true. No amount of wishing it hadn't happened would unshoot that gun, would unravel that man's actions back into his car and away from Trousdale; no amount of hoping would lead him this way or that out of his childhood or undo whatever it was that led him to that horrendous day. We all have choices. To blame what happened on a childhood or on a mental illness is to deny those choices. Because if he'd had no choice but to end up in Trousdale that night, then what does it matter if you (or I) do the right thing or the wrong thing? What's the point, if it's all out of our control in any case?

Off-loading blame depends on a view of the universe that simply doesn't jibe with my own—this was true well before my mother's murder. God wills things, God has a hand in everything, but he also gives us free will, gives us choice, gives us the power to be better, by his grace, than we thought we could be. The Bible tells us, "No temptation has overtaken you except such as is common to man; but God is faithful, who will not allow you to be tempted beyond what you are able, but with the temptation will also make the way of escape, that you may be able to bear it" (1 Corinthians 10:13). A way of escape—that's what God gives us always and in every situation. But if we choose to see the world as preordained, with no diverging paths or means of escape, then nothing will ever be made whole.

After the death of my mother, I kept thinking of the message in Proverbs 16:9: "A man's heart plans his way, but the Lord directs his steps." How was I going to devise my way? What was I going to choose to see each and every day? Would I give the man who did this to us anything beyond forgiveness? As Bishop Jakes had asked me, would I choose to focus on those few minutes in which Mom's killer devastated our family, or would I think of the eighty-one years of my mother's life, and the unknowable amount of time I had left with my father?

There were practical concerns, too. I had calls to make; there were detectives and lawyers to deal with. *It is what it is; what was I going to do about it?* Well, for a start, I wasn't going to shirk any calls . . . until sometimes I did! Once in a while I'd say, "I'm not going to do anything for the next two hours. I'm going to go take a bath, and then I'm going to take a nap." But that was later; December was all action. The holidays were lovely, oddly—perhaps because my mom had loved Christmas, we were able to appreciate the holidays as a time of remembrance and joy and renewal. Life continues, I knew that; and what did I choose to see? Well, knowing how much she loved Christmas presented me with a choice: Would I not put up a tree, for example, because she was no longer with us—or would I put up an even bigger tree, pay attention to it more than usual, maybe find things from her house that I could put on the tree, to make sure it was as special as possible, was *her* tree?

Of course I did the latter. I wanted to walk into the room and see a huge tree filled with memories of my mother.

I was also using meditation to mitigate the trauma and stress at that time, as a sort of insurance policy against breaking down. The shock the world had felt for us had lessened by the time the new year approached—so much so that by Christmas we were back to a tight inner circle. By around January 1, the world naturally started to turn its mind away from what had happened to the Avants. The shock and trauma and stress may have stayed at a high level for us, but for others they waned.

Ted told me he'd get calls suggesting I was in denial because I hadn't broken hard. "No," he'd say with a laugh, "that's just Nicole. She's built like a freakin' tank." (Poor choice of words, Ted!) But still he could hear in people's voices a dubiousness, as though we were going through pure hell and just not telling anyone. Well, we were going through hell, but we were also choosing to move forward.

"This is her way," Ted told people. "This is her faith in action."

It was true: at all times, I was standing in my faith, as

noted earlier. That stance doesn't mean things are always fun, doesn't mean things are pretty or easy, but I was determined to stand in an energy of faith.

What I mean by "energy of faith" is this: I didn't and still don't understand any of what's going on; I don't like how any of it feels. In fact, it often feels horrible. But instead of being paralyzed by my mother's death and its repercussions, I am calling on the grace and the comfort of the universe to step in and work through me.

Meanwhile, as I've said, everyone was waiting for me to fall apart at any moment. But I think a lot of people forgot that I had my elderly father to take care of. It was a bit like having a child in the house; he had needs that I couldn't have predicted, and I had to keep him safe and fed and occupied.

I've noticed that my father, in the face of the unimaginable, when no amount of life experience (and he's had more than most) offers answers for what has been wrought upon him, has taken to creating repetitive strategies, as if the habitual might hold back the torrent of what cannot be understood. In the drawer by his bed, for instance, he keeps paper napkins, nearly one hundred of them, perfectly cut into squares, folded just so—and he knows if even one is missing. Out in the garden, many days we sit and just count planes together, imagining where each aircraft is headed, who is up there, looking down on just the two of us.

I, too, have trained my brain to go someplace other than grief, someplace where we're not at the bottom of a pit. When Dad does his exercises in the yard, I do them with him. We watch TV reruns together, too. Sometimes we watch *Blue Bloods* on Paramount Plus or *Chicago Fire* on Peacock. (Ted "Netflix" Sarandos has to show us how to find those channels on our TV.)

Basically, we do whatever it takes for a new way of life to be established, one that keeps the horror away.

Sometimes, Ted will sit with Dad and watch the crows land on the lawn. "Look at that motherfucker," Dad says, referring, I think, to the crows, not Ted.

That's the laughter we try to keep in this house.

But sometimes we can't hold back the outside world and its need for answers we don't have.

One evening a few months after Mom's death, we attended an event at the Wallis Annenberg Center for the Performing Arts to honor some friends. Unfortunately, many people came up to ask my dad for details about what had happened, and to say, "How could this happen to our Jacquie?"—as though he, or anyone, had any answers; some even cried hysterically in his presence.

"Listen, guys," I said. "Here's the deal. You know how people say, 'Just pull the Band-Aid off'? This is different. Just imagine that we recently had open-heart surgery, and we have stitches that are brand new, and every time you ask for details, you're going in and pulling some stitches out."

Someone explained that they were just trying to wrap their head around what had happened. I get it, I do; but if *we* can't wrap our heads around it, and instead are choosing to move forward in grace and motion . . . ? The truth is, there *are* no answers. And that is what we must learn to live with, if we can. In the end, there was nothing to be done that evening—we had to leave early. Now, when we're out, often Dad will say to me, "Do you think we'll have to leave early again because people will come and want to talk about Jacquie?" It breaks my heart every time.

A simple *I love you*, or *I'm here for you*, or *I'm praying for you*—all these work like a charm. They're healing balms; especially *I love you*. The worse the trauma, the less you say—that's a really good lesson that I've had to learn myself. For a start, no one knows what to say—how could they?

What I'm getting at here is the importance of shifting our energy and seeing each other—I mean, really *seeing* each other. Seeing is the magic that comes from fully embracing the person in front of you, engaging honestly with them, caring about what's happening in their life. But *really seeing* comes only from a change of energy. Seeing is giving away one's sense of superiority and letting the other person steal the limelight. It's seeing that someone is making their way the only way they know how. Seeing is how we connect, deeply, with each other. And maybe seeing each other will help prevent what happened to my family from happening again.

When you know you're loved, you can more easily love others. As 1 Peter 4:8 urges us: "Above all things have fervent love for one another, for 'love will cover a multitude of sins.'"

And by *love* I don't mean the soft-focus, Hallmark kind; I mean the kind that looks beyond the surface into a sense of greater purpose. I mean the love that Ruby Bridges had for her country, and the love Ruby Bridges's parents had for their daughter, even when it cost them everything.

◆ ◆ ◆

Ruby Bridges was the eldest of five children. Her parents, Abon and Lucille, were farmers who moved to New Orleans to chase a better life for their family.

In 1960, schools in Louisiana were ordered to desegregate. That year, Ruby Bridges became the first African American to desegregate the school nearest to her house, William Frantz Elementary School, an otherwise all-white school. Ruby was spit on as she walked in, she was called the N-word, and the other children were pulled out of class. Ruby was given leave to bring her own lunch to school, as there had been threats to poison her, and she spent a year being taught by one of the only teachers who would do so, a white woman named Barbara Henry. Federal marshals were dispatched to keep Ruby safe as she and her mother walked to school each day.

Ruby was six years old.

Ruby Bridges survived all this, and prospered, though not before her father lost his job, her mother was refused service in local stores, and Ruby's grandparents were turned off their sharecropping land. Her act of extraordinary bravery—she had perfect attendance that year (despite having to eat lunch alone in fear)—caused a firestorm of prejudice to break over New Orleans.

Things were difficult for Ruby later in life, too—she would lose her house in Hurricane Katrina. And yet she would fight for William Frantz Elementary School to stay open, even after all it had done to her.

Ruby Bridges is just thirteen years older than I am. If it weren't for her, I don't know what sort of life I would have had. President Obama said the same thing to her at the White House in 2011 as they looked at the iconic Normal Rockwell painting *The Problem We All Live With*, which depicts what she had to go through.

Obama said, "I think it's fair to say that if it hadn't been for you guys, I might not be here, and we wouldn't be looking at this together."

My mother used to say, "See what Ruby did? She was six years old. She wasn't trying to integrate a school. She was just going to kindergarten. She was getting called the N-word, she was being spit on. Aren't you glad that she didn't quit? Aren't you grateful to her?"

That was the sort of gratitude my mother taught me to hold dear and close in my heart. Her point was that everyone has the chance to sow a seed. Sometimes you get the harvest in your lifetime and sometimes you don't, but you have to focus on the seed. You sow that seed through your daily actions, and through the purity of your thoughts, the sanctity of your words. Hopefully, the seed that you're planting will bear fruit not only for you, but also for others. But if it's never for you? You just go on sowing the righteous way. As Ecclesiastes 11:6 has it, "In the morning sow your seed, and in the evening do not withhold your hand; for you do not know which will prosper, either this or that, or whether both alike will be good."

◆ ◆ ◆

Sacrificing something wonderful is always hard; and sacrificing to better the world, at the expense of our own ease or safety is harder still. Consider the case of Jesse Owens in the 1936 Summer Olympics in Berlin, winning four gold medals for the United States in front of Hitler, standing up to his tyrannical racism with power and grace. How terrified Jesse must have been, and yet fear didn't stop him performing to his greatest potential. Not for Ruby, not for Jesse, the myth of being triggered into surrender; they just did the right thing in the face of enormous fear and intimidation. (Some athletes now step away from competition when they're mentally not ready to perform, and I'm glad for that focus on mental health now. But this was different. I can't imagine anyone being more terrified than Jesse Owens at those Olympics, and yet he *was* ready; he performed even when it could have meant losing his freedom or even his life.)

We need to be able to see the blessings we have been afforded and then cause those blessings to inform our own bravery. For all the sweetness of icing, it would be nothing without the cake that underlies it. Because we today are merely passing a baton in this life, it is essential that we educate ourselves as to what our forebears sacrificed for us. I was born one month before the death of Dr. Martin Luther King Jr. My father helped the King movement pay for hotel rooms, food, transportation—whatever was needed in the aftermath. With me still a brand-new baby, my mother begged my father to not attend the funeral—she was terrified my dad wouldn't come back. But he went anyway; the baton was being passed, even in the darkest hour. That is why, I think, I'm able to not waste a day wondering at the unfairness of what happened to Jacqueline Avant. It is what it is; what am I going to do about it? Shall I get involved and stand up for what I think is right, or shall I call in sick with mental health days for the rest of my life?

Recently, I found myself once again praying for divine timing. (I'm always asking the Divine for something, be it divine order, divine timing, divine grace.) I was working on producing a movie, but I felt that the project was moving too slowly. I got the sense that others on the team thought, because it was just three months after my mother died, that it would be unseemly to push too hard. But that's what I wanted to do: the story of the movie was too important to stall. It concerns the 850 Black women of the 6888th Central Postal Directory Battalion, unsung heroes whom I mentioned in an earlier chapter. That battalion, also known as the Six Triple Eight, worked to clear a three-year backlog of mail during World War II to bolster the morale of men serving abroad.

I happened to be calling Tyler Perry about something else, and during the course of that conversation, my intuition led me to discuss the project about those hardworking women from the Six Triple Eight. I just knew that this was in some way *his* project; he had to tell the story, and it was my job to convince him to take it on.

Now, the story of those incredible women from the Six Triple Eight will be passed on to a new generation so that we can all relearn the perspective that the Greatest Generation bequeathed us: that doing something for the greater good matters more than how we feel on any given day.

◆ ◆ ◆

But it's not just at the macro level—the Ruby Bridges / Jesse Owens world-altering level—that truly *seeing* each other is a crucial endeavor. We're called every day to be witnesses to each other. We just need to remember to look up from our damn phones!

Recently, I was in line at a supermarket. Ahead of me was a woman, and let's just say that nothing she was wearing made sense; there were greens and reds and pinks and blues and sweaters and scarves. I wasn't feeling superior to her—I've seen myself in the mirror before the day begins, and it's nothing to write home about—but there was certainly something going on with this woman that day.

The more I looked at her, the more my heart filled, though; she seemed like someone who dressed that way because she was used to being unseen.

Looking at her, I thought about how close to the border of loneliness and oblivion we all are, especially now that no one looks up from their devices. And I felt something akin to sorrow for her, but also recognition. I'm lucky that I have people who care about me, but you never know what's coming in this world.

So that day in the supermarket, the feeling of needing to do something grew and grew; I knew I had to act on purpose, with kindness. Suddenly, a voice inside of me said, "Tell her that her earrings are pretty. Tell her. Go on. Tell her."

But no—who was I to do such a thing? Yet this phrase kept coming into my head: "Tell her that her earrings are pretty."

We're called every day to be witnesses to each other. We just need to remember to look up from our damn phones!

Still I hesitated—until she turned around and looked at me. Meeting her eyes, I said, "I think your earrings are really pretty."

Her eyes filled with tears, as did mine.

There was a tiny shift in the universe right then. I felt it, and I'm pretty sure she felt it, too. She grabbed at the earrings and said, "These? Oh my God. I made them for my grandmother when I was really young. They were her favorites. I loved my grandmother so much. But she died recently, and I'm empty without her."

Then she said, "I can't believe you noticed them. No one else ever has. Now I know that my grandmother is looking out for me."

We maintained eye contact, and I think we both recognized that we'd given each other a tiny gift, but also something vast and important.

And that was it—she bought her groceries, I bought mine, and I headed out to my car. I got in the driver's seat and thought about our interaction. Suddenly I found myself crying, because I realized that the way she'd looked at me had made it clear: no one had ever really seen her; no one had ever truly looked at her. No one. And that's what I'd been called to do.

Why had no one ever seen her? Why had no damned person ever mentioned her freaking earrings?

I was reminded then, all over again, that we desperately need to see each other: it's urgent. For so long, Black men, and Black women, and women generally have been invisible.

If you try to make everyone around you visible—the woman being accosted in the alleyway, the woman in the store with the earrings, even the kids whose parents just honk the horn at a playdate pickup and drive away without going inside to say hi—that's how you make sure that love is visible. This is important for everyone, but I think it's especially important for Black people in America. We have always felt invisible in our own country. No matter how smart we are, no matter if we're scientists or doctors or writers or athletes or musicians, too often we don't get the proper credit; or we get death threats; or we get pulled over, pulled out, pushed to the ground, beaten up, or worse. Imagine this: even with everyone filming everything on their phones these days, clear violations of civil rights and human rights go unpunished; now ask yourself what it was like before cell phones. You don't have to be a bleeding-heart liberal to understand that our society is not based on fairness and equal treatment under the law.

The injustice goes so deep—so very, very deep. Black people have seldom gotten credit for their inventions, their talent; they just weren't seen. So we've often had to reinvent ourselves using mind over matter: Quincy told me recently that he arranged the score to "Fly Me to the Moon" so many times that there was no way that Frank Sinatra could say no to it. (He also reminded me that "Fly Me to the Moon" was the first song ever played on the actual moon!)

It makes me think of Ernest Withers (no relation to Bill!), the man who took an iconic photograph on March 28,

1968, during the Memphis sanitation workers' strike, in which the protestors are holding up signs that read "I <u>AM</u> A MAN." (I was sad to later find out that Ernest also took photos of protesters and fed them to the FBI.)

But boy, that underlining of <u>AM</u>—that hits home hard. These brave souls had to argue the fact that they were human, let alone in need of rights and protections like everyone in America. Each of the men depicted was somebody's child, somebody's partner, somebody's friend, and they were doing the right thing on the streets of Memphis simply because it had to be done; they expected no prize for it. They wanted merely to be *seen*. They believed in the American Dream—probably more passionately than their white brethren, truth be told—and wanted to make it reality. It's easy to think you're living a dream if you're awake in ease; it's much harder to do so when none of your dreams seems within reach. And yet Black folks continue to believe in the best of the culture that treats them so poorly.

That's why, when I'm out for dinner and someone doesn't treat the staff with respect? Oh boy. One night in particular, years ago, I was on a date, and I thought I was actually going to like the guy until he was incredibly rude to the waitress.

"Wait," I said, "*what* did you just say to her?"

The guy looked at me as though I were making way too big a deal of it. "That's somebody's child," I said.

♦ ♦ ♦

I believe in the power of paying it forward, because when you do well, you feel good; and when you feel good, your vibration becomes higher; and others then want to follow. In other words, success and feeling good are contagious.

I'm all about positive contagious vibrations!

But sometimes I go too far.

December 1, 2022, loomed large: it would be the first anniversary of my mother's death. It was a day I dreaded. For weeks before, good-hearted people had been in touch, wanting to talk to me about what was coming up, how they felt, how I felt . . . it was too much. I prayed for some kind of divine intervention, hoping that my mother would come up with something from beyond the grave that might make the day bearable.

She never lets me down.

A few days before the anniversary, Ted came home from work and said, "You know how much you love President Macron?" He likes to tease me about this, but it's true. I think that the eighth president of the Fifth Republic of France is utterly fantastic. I love his vibe, his erudition, his extraordinary love story (marrying his high-school French and Latin teacher thirteen years after they met, for crying out loud)—*everything*. Everyone around me knows that I'm a huge fan of Emmanuel Macron, including, it seems, his closest advisors.

"There's going to be a state dinner in Washington," Ted said. "Macron's people know you're a big fan. We're invited."

"Yes!" I said. "When?"

"That's the best part," Ted said. "December 1."

The night of the dinner, I could barely contain my excitement. I donned my favorite pieces of Mom's jewelry in her honor, and off we went to the White House, where the black-tie dinner would be celebrated in a huge tent on the South Lawn. Before we sat down to dine, there was the obligatory receiving line. By the time we neared our turn to greet President Biden and the first lady, along with President Macron and his wife, Brigitte, I was still trying to decide what I'd say.

"Ted, should I say, 'President Macron, you are a wonderful world leader,' or would it be better to simply say, 'You are one of the best presidents France has ever had'? What do you think, Ted? Tell me!"

By this point, I was basically six years old. Ted, because he was aware, as I was, of the extraordinary flukes of life that had come together to make our presence at the White House happen, and knew also that this was exactly the gift I needed from the universe—well, Ted just smiled at me with a mixture of amusement and what I now realize was not a little fear. (And surely if this kind of serendipity could happen on this date, things would be fine eventually.)

By the time we reached the Bidens and the Macrons, I was filled with so much joy and excitement that I basically forgot I was a former United States ambassador. I had been to diplomat school—I should know how to do this—but in fact I was there as a fan, almost a stan! (Barack Obama had taught me how to remain calm firsthand, too—he'd just flick his shoulder as though getting rid of something irritating and tell me to simply relax and respond, not get too excited and overreact. But this was no time to be Obamian!)

Finally, it was our turn. As I shook President Biden's hand and greeted him, out of the corner of my eye I could see President Macron, and that was enough for me. Dropping Joe Biden's hand as if it were on fire, I turned to the French president, and in front of the president of the United States, the first lady, Brigitte Macron, and my husband, I got my two greetings mixed up:

"You should be the president of the world!" I exclaimed.

You know that moment when everything goes quiet and the earth stops, just a little, hiccups on its axis before regaining its usual spin? That's what happened then. Macron did his best to be decorous—"Madame, *enchanté*," he said, backing up just enough, I imagine, to be sure his protective service had a clear path to wrestle me to the ground. But his wife looked stricken; and God knows what the president of the United States thought about a former ambassador advocating, in front of him (right before a state dinner, no less), that his job as leader of our great nation should be subsumed under some kind of universal presidency—Macron as a sort of all-powerful global overlord, the mere idea of which millions had fought so valiantly to vanquish during World War II.

Somewhere from beyond I could hear my mother saying, "Nicole! Where are your manners?" But I could hear her laughter, too, there, on the anniversary of the worst day imaginable, now made infinitely more bearable by the creation, in my mind at least, of a political appointment for which I would be more than happy to open my address book.

A few minutes later Ted and I found ourselves in a room off to the side of the main banquet hall and burst into laughter—deep, gusty belly laughs.

"Happy" was not an emotion I'd expected ever to feel again on December 1. But there Ted and I were, in a room next to a collection of the most powerful people on earth, howling. We laughed so hard that my mascara began to melt. I didn't care—in that moment, I was truly happy.

* * *

I can't stress it enough: a crucial part of my parents' legacy has been to make sure that no one was ever going to be invisible.

That's why my father championed Bill Withers so hard, as just one example. (I don't think I mentioned that Bill was the youngest of six kids from Slab Fork, West Virginia, a town of two hundred in the poor southwest corner of one of the poorest states. Talk about invisible!) As we saw earlier, Bill had been turned down by everyone he'd approached, and he was expecting the same from my dad. As for my dad, well, he'd been handling Joe Glaser's clients, and Bill was my father's own to make. It was lucky that both Bill and Clarence were ready when the time came. Bill had the songs—boy, did he have the songs!—and my dad had the connections.

And my mother, too, wanted to make sure that people were seen, were provided for, were loved, no matter where they came from.

This is what we're all called to do—not just Clarence, not just Jacqueline, not just me, not just you . . . *all* of us. We are called every day to *see* each other—to see each person's humanity before we see any differences. So whenever you find yourself in a situation where you wonder if a particular person has been seen, just do one thing:

Notice the effing earrings.

AFTERMATH

After seven days, we sat shiva.

Each of my friends blessed me with something—a book of psalms, Joan Didion's *The Year of Magical Thinking*, crystals, poems. As we went around the table, everyone shared an offering.

During those early days, people would call me or write me to tell me the hell they were going through over my mother's death, and I just tuned them out. I thought, "I have an elderly father living with me now, who just lost his wife. And I have tons of things to do. I'm planning the funeral."

Then I realized that I didn't even know where her body was. Detectives were calling with questions, police were calling with updates—I said, "Wait, wait, wait. Where's my mom's body?"

I was doing okay—keeping busy, pushing the reason for my busy-ness into the background—until my friend Will showed up. I hadn't known he was coming, but suddenly there he was. He'd met my mom only a couple of times, but he had tears in his eyes. Seeing him standing there, looking shocked and teary, I broke too, falling into his arms.

It was too much.

Aftermath

I was born on my mother's twenty-eighth birthday. Which must have sucked for her, to be honest. But as the years went by, it cemented the connection we had.

On March 6, 2022, we went to Mom's gravesite—Ted, my brother, and I. I hadn't planned anything particular, but as we stood there on my own birthday, I felt moved to sing "Happy Birthday" to my mom.

From there we made the rounds of various establishments in Los Angeles—the Polo Lounge, the Peninsula, the Beverly Hills Hotel—and in every one, we found a gang of my mom's friends having tea in tribute to her. They'd gotten together to grieve, to remember, to laugh, to honor.

That day was tough, but the biggest test of my life was looming.

There would be a trial. I was dreading it, as was my father: he couldn't get it out of his head; it was keeping him awake and fretful. Once again, I think my mother somehow got involved, because the killer eventually pleaded no contest to all the charges. Suddenly, no trial. Underestimating my mother has never worked for anyone. I looked up at the heavens after learning of his plea, and I . . . wondered.

Try to be kind to everyone you meet because everyone is fighting their own battle, and you don't know what that battle is, or what it's taking out of them.

As I was driving home from the hospital that first morning, I stopped at a red light. "Oh my God, wait, is this really happening?" I thought. "Did my dad just become a widower?" As I sat there, the light must have changed to green, because behind me some guy was blaring his horn at me.

I didn't get mad. I froze in deep sadness and just waved an apology into my rearview mirror and drove on. But if I'd stopped that guy and told him what had just happened, what then? I suspect he would have regretted his honking.

No one ever knows what anyone is going through. So tread lightly.

Later, I'd be asked to submit a victim impact statement to the court. This is what I wrote . . . and oh, I didn't tread lightly:

Aftermath

NICOLE ALEXANDRA AVANT

March 30, 2022

Dear Judge,

There are no words to describe the nightmare we have endured because of the cruel and vicious acts of the defendant.

As I write this letter, painfully reflecting on the shocking horror of that night and the emotional and psychological aftermath that has followed, there is only one word that describes the state of our family: *shattered*.

We are shattered.

Jacqueline Avant, our beloved mother and wife, was very much alive, and she loved her life. She was vibrant, she was active, and she was a critical support beam for her family, her many friends, and the communities she served. My mother devoted every cell in her body to helping others, spending over thirty years as an organizer, activist, and advocate for the people, and more specifically, the children of Watts.

To have her life brutally taken from us and the

countless people who depended on her support, love, and generosity is devastating, and we will suffer from not only her loss, but also how it occurred, for the rest of our lives.

Nobody who lived the way she did should have had to die the way she died.

Second to her faith, my mother's greatest belief was in the possibility of a safe and just world, and this is why we ask that the defendant spend the rest of his natural life in prison, without the possibility of parole.

We will never get my mother back, but we feel it is our duty to act in her footsteps and work to protect the people in our communities. The trauma we are living through is immeasurable; we have no idea what healing from this violent loss looks like or if it is even possible, but we hold on to the hope that this individual will never have the chance to do this to another family.

Sincerely,
Nicole Avant and the Avant-Sarandos Family

TEN

The Magic of Seeing

Thank you, Jacquie, for your gifts of
intuition, courage, patience, tenacity,
and your most precious gift to us:
love. You helped us to be fearless in
a landscape of adversity.

So, she's in surgery?" I asked when I arrived in the waiting
room on the night I received the terrible phone call.

"Yes," someone said, "she's been in for half an hour."

This is how the desperate-for-hope mind works: I thought,
"Okay, good—she was alive when she got to Cedars; otherwise they wouldn't perform surgery." Just to make sure, I
confirmed that she'd still been alive when she arrived. This,
then, seemed to be an immense piece of good news.

After a while, hospital staff called us into a room with some privacy. It was just like the movies, though it wasn't a movie. Then multiple doctors trooped in; they just looked at us.

The doctors used a lot of words—we did this, we did that, there was a lot of blood—until Ted finally said, "I think I know what you're saying, but can you actually say the words? Did she make it or not?"

"We're very sorry," one of the surgeons said. "She didn't make it." I sat upright; my father fell on me; my brother wailed like a pierced beast.

I never said to myself, "Mom died." I think I knew intuitively what had happened, but the words that came to me were "She *left*."

On the way out of the hospital, I tried to explain to my father what had happened.

"She didn't make it through the surgery, Dad," I said. "They tried, but she just didn't make it through."

In his shock he simply said, "Oh . . . okay."

There was no understanding to be had in the small hours of a hospital parking lot, so I told my brother's girlfriend to look after my brother, and Ted to drive my father with us to our home.

In that moment I said to myself, "Now I'm Superwoman. Now I'm Wonder Woman." My mother had always been my superhero; now I had to be my own. She had given me the tools, fortunately. I was horribly sad that I had to use them without her, but that didn't mean I didn't intend to use them to the very best of my ability. Yes, even then, at the starkest moment of my life, I knew I had the strength, the grit, to raise myself and others up. I was tremendously grateful for the grace she had given me.

As I walked to the car, I repeated this prayer: "[I am] strong in the Lord and in the power of His might." This passage from Ephesians 6 is one I've always loved. The passage goes on to ask that "I may open my mouth boldly to make known the mystery of the gospel, for which I am an ambassador," which seems appropriate for me.

I repeated those words from Ephesians over and over and over that morning, as I've done many times since. Though they're scripture, they feel, too, like words my mother imprinted on me throughout my life. After all, all the way back in high school Mom had won for service in her yearbook— she could have won all the prizes ("Most Dignified," "Literary Lights," on and on), but no surprise, Jacqueline Gray won under the heading "Done Most for Adams." After the murders of Andrew Goodman, James Chaney, and Michael Schwerner in the summer of 1964, something changed for her: she was still determined to live a life of service, yes, but also one of strength and power. This is the woman who just four years later would give birth to me. She was gone now, but she was also *not* gone.

A couple of nights after her death, a group of my friends from childhood came over to my house. (Many of them had known me since I was five years old.) It was a night in which stories were told about my mother, about my father, about growing up together . . . and in all that, there was one common theme: Jacqueline Avant never spoke to those kids as though they were stupid little children. "She always talked to us as people," one friend said. Another said, "She always had a smile on her face"; someone else described her as "strict and orderly, but fun."

"Yeah, you could have fun," one friend added, "but you just couldn't be an asshole."

"She used to pick us up from bowling . . ."

"From soccer . . ."

It was as if we were hailing her at her next birthday party, or at a fundraiser or a gala event at which she was the guest of honor. It was as if she were there.

That's because she *was* there.

• • •

When I sold my mom's car after she died, it basically had zero miles on it—she'd always stayed pretty close to home, deeply embedded in the community around her. After her death we would get letters of condolence from random places. Someone in the shoe department at Neiman Marcus started her letter, "You never met me . . ." and went on to extol the kindness of my mother. Same thing from a Whole Foods checkout person: "I saw Ms. Avant every week . . ." My parents attended the Wallis Annenberg Center for the Performing Arts probably three nights a week; she was on their board, too, and had been integral in the center's founding and existence. When my mother turned eighty and we had a party, she made a point of no gifts. "I want donations made to the Wallis," she said. "Put that on the invitation."

The most common thread in all the notes we received was that my mother *saw* people. She'd often jot a note or leave a voicemail or send a text to check in on her friends. "How are you?" she'd say or write. "I was just thinking about you." She was very intuitive, people reported; she always knew what someone needed. Didn't matter if you were family, or the gas station attendant; people were people, and Mom made sure they knew that they mattered.

◆ ◆ ◆

In March 2021, my mother and I had what would be our last joint birthday celebration together. It can be hard after five decades of knowing someone, being raised by someone, looking after someone, to break through with that person, to find new words to say, healing words, words that would be both true but also kind. But that lunch was a watershed for my mother and me.

The conversation we'd had a quarter century earlier—the one inspired by her reading of Louise Hay, which hadn't gone entirely as I'd hoped it would—seemed to linger over our table. Our shared birthday always brought an intensity to each passing year; and in 2021, old wounds were about to be healed.

"I've had a lot of time to think during COVID," my mother said at one point. "And I think I understand some things better now. Back in the early days, when you were young, it was very important to your father and me that we created a safe place for artists to land—they were difficult times. That safe place just so happened to be our house, the one you grew up in. This was a choice I made, along with your dad. But all these years later, I do want to apologize that I didn't acknowledge your feelings about it."

Clearly that earlier conversation had stuck with her, too.

It's important to understand that she wasn't apologizing for her choice; rather, she was sorry for how she'd responded to me when the subject came up.

Then she said, "But I do think I was a very good mother." (The moxie of her; what a character!)

She went on: "I do think you turned out very well, by the way. And don't forget, my mother didn't hug me until I was seventeen, right after my father died. Early on, I was afraid I was making you into a friend. Someone told me that wasn't a good idea. My job was to raise you—there had to be a boundary. I couldn't care less if you liked me. My job was to make you thrive and respond well in the world and to the world. If I'm your best friend and everything is always okay, well, then I haven't done my job.

"Every generation is supposed to do better than the next. I know I did better than Zella did, and Zella did better than her mother. In any case, you had the life of a princess—a very comfortable existence—and the last thing I wanted was to rear someone who couldn't deal with the world. I had to give you your roadmap, help you shape your plan, point you in the right direction. I needed to be able to look at myself in the mirror and feel all right when the day was done. You needed grit, and it was my job to make sure you developed it. I didn't want you to be always worried about your feelings. No one can function productively like that.

"You owe the world the best version of yourself. You owe it to those who suffered for you. There's this door open that's never been open before, and I couldn't let you walk through it and go on to mess up."

My mother paused to sip her wine and reflect.

"I did what I could for my family," she concluded. "I kept the whole thing running. And I showed up for you."

My mom also apologized for her "look"—the look she often gave me when she was disappointed in me or when I had missed the mark. Her look scared the hell out of me—out of all of us. We referred to it as the "Joan Crawford/Wicked Witch of the West" look, and it pierced right through my heart and always made me feel less than good enough.

But at that last birthday lunch, my mom showed up in a different light, with soft, kind eyes, and deeply apologized to me for ever making me feel small or ashamed. She told me that her purpose with the look was to let me know that my behavior was wrong and inappropriate, but never my soul—and that she realized many years later that that was too hard of a lesson for a young child to comprehend. What she'd wanted for me was to show up for myself. She was very big on discipline and integrity because she felt they'd lead to a sense of personal responsibility, which then would lead to personal integrity, which would hopefully help me keep my word to and for myself.

I always had the will to do things, but my mom was committed to showing me the how, and her look was meant to be a signpost, even when it looked more like a stop sign.

When I was a child, her look felt as if I was constantly being crucified; as an adult, I now know it was an opportunity for a resurrection to occur in my soul. A resurrection always follows a crucifixion if we allow the purpose to unfold.

This gift she gave me is one that I will cherish throughout eternity.

My mother had spoken at that lunch without rancor or bitterness; she was simply stating facts as she saw them.

I excused myself for a moment, wanting a second to think about the right response. In the bathroom, I looked in the mirror and said, "I knew it!" I felt a mixture of relief and shock; finally, I knew I wasn't crazy. I was grateful she had acknowledged her approach to childrearing—but I also realized she wasn't sorry for pushing me in the way she had. And I could now see that what I'd thought had been selfishness had in fact been the opposite.

Back at the table, her honest words gave birth to mine, words I'd longed to say for so long.

"Mom," I said, "thank you for acknowledging that my feelings were hurt when we first discussed this all those years ago."

She nodded. "My reaction wasn't very kind," she said. "I pinched your heart."

"I'm taking the love and the lessons and leaving the rest behind," I said. "We just came through a pandemic—all is forgiven, and I don't care about the bullshit. You helped me get to where I am today—so it's a wrap. All is forgiven. It's a complicated relationship only until it's not. And today I declare that it's not complicated."

My mom sighed with what I took to be great relief and thanked me for lifting that burden with forgiveness.

Perhaps the best part about our final birthday lunch was that it was an intersection of our truths, and this time those truths didn't collide. We had found a way to accept and acknowledge the other's true feelings, and we did it with more love and understanding than ever before.

I had been able to show up with the perspective and the mind of an adult and finally accept her reasons, her truth, and she had been able to soften her heart and allow my truth in too, and honor it with her wisdom.

Mom looked me in my eyes and said, "I love you, Nicole. Thank you."

Then we had cake and blew out candles and basked in the knowledge of the love we had for each other.

That's what forgiveness is: getting rid of the heaviness, poison, and burdens we suffer under, and giving all that to God to carry for us.

So now I'm grieving with hope. My mom is in my future.

♦ ♦ ♦

My mother raised me up in the company of victorious people whom I admired for their moral courage and moral strength. I am the promise of a people denied their God-given freedom to pursue their own happiness; and in turn, my promise is to share my blessings with people who deserve to receive them.

How we respond to trouble determines our destiny and our outcome. This is true whether we're born impoverished and unlucky or born into a life of opportunity. Our underlying beliefs are more determinative of our future than are our circumstances. Due to my parents' example and convictions, I believe in grit, gratitude, and grace. I believe that a strong soul leads to a sound mind. I believe in cultivating a sacred heart. These have been my grounding principles in life—and they remain so, even after everything.

I have realized over and over again that the only way out is *through*.

And glorifying God has kept me blessed, content, and protected. I'm anchored in hope, and by a fervent faith in the Divine: Jesus. Mother Mary, God. Everything that is good.

Yes, even after everything.

We can't quit on ourselves; we have to keep pruning, have to keep looking at ourselves and working out how we can improve, what we can get involved in, whom we can better love today.

And while sadness and loss are a given in any fully lived life, misery is always optional. We shouldn't get stuck at the point of our pain; we have to shake it off.

We have to make sure that whatever we say after the words "I am . . ." is exactly as we want it to be, because there is a law of the universe that brings life out of words and intentions. Followed correctly, that law will never steer us wrong. Romans 4:17 says, "God . . . gives life to the dead and calls those things which do not exist as though they did"; while Proverbs 4:23 advises, "Keep your heart with all diligence, for out of it spring the issues of life."

While sadness and loss are a given in any fully lived life, misery is always optional.

My grandmother used to follow me around her house saying, "[Whoever] believes those things he says will be done, he will have whatever he says" (Mark 11:23).

In other words, what I speak is made real. So I'm extremely careful about what I say after I say, "I am . . ."

And it's not just our words. How do we behave, play, show up, learn, sacrifice? All this determines the legacy we leave. No one else can determine that for us. We are all responsible for our energy and what it accomplishes.

If we want to do good, that energy needs to be positive. In 1 Thessalonians 5:18, we hear, "In everything give thanks; for this is the will of God in Christ Jesus for you." I've found things to be glad about and grateful for even after the loss of my mother. We need to make the pain count. This is what I'm doing with my pain—making it count for something good by transforming it into positive energy.

As I said at the outset, I believe that positivity breeds positivity. The seeds we plant determine the nature of our harvest. Optimism and hope make us invaluable. Hope is an aggressively positive frame of mind, and I choose to be anchored in hope.

As for me, well, I am the ruler of my emotions. I expect something good every day. Negative thoughts and actions take more energy than positive ones do in any case, so why not pick the positive?

Using that positive energy, I'm speaking my truth into existence. Never underestimate the power of setting an intention with words. Many of us remember the lines from the book of Joel: "Beat your plowshares into swords, and your pruning hooks into spears," but the next line is crucial, too: "Let the weak say, 'I *am* strong'" (3:10).

We must focus on creating a life worth living, a valuable dash between our birthdate and our end. Do it aggressively, with hope.

Keep getting up. Keep saying yes.

+ + +

This must be our regular question: "What does this terrible or tragic thing make possible?" Turn your perspective around: this is happening *for* me, not *to* me. We must endeavor to bring persistence, fortitude, and perseverance to everything we do. Don't forget to praise. Give glory. Share any honor—better yet, give all honor away.

Whatever we do, we should do with humility. Humility is not thinking less of yourself; it's thinking of yourself less.

+ + +

How did I get to this moment today?

It took a lot of courage, sacrifice, prayer, and love on the part of other people to allow me to be who I am today. I will never be able to thank all those people personally, but I can live my thank-you by creating a good and decent life, serving others, and enjoying the blessings bestowed upon me.

I think of all of them now, all those people enslaved, who

were treated as second-class citizens. I think of the sacrifice that the abolitionists also made—Black and white—all those freedom fighters.

They've passed me the baton, and I must now run my race.

✦ ✦ ✦

People today have become discontent, are out of sorts. We don't seem to remember that life is a gift. We've given ourselves away to strangers; we've grown so concerned about how many "likes" we receive from those strangers that we miss the opportunities given to us daily to truly connect with the person next to

Keep getting up. Keep saying yes.

us. But we human beings *must* connect; it's in our nature. We must smile at each other, laugh with each other, cry with each other, support each other, and look out for each other.

A better way forward begins and ends with respecting one another. I do my best to live by the principle of the Golden Rule—treat others as you yourself wish to be treated—and when I stray from that rule, I come back to center and start again, because God's mercy is new every day. Following the Golden Rule doesn't mean we're never going to disappoint people; it's about the *how* of doing something, the intention, and not just the outcome.

But we always have a choice—we are merely God's co-authors. We can think, imagine, and believe whatever we want to—so why not think, imagine, and believe the way God does?

We mustn't forget to worship God even when we're in the storm. We must give praise even when we don't feel like it. We must do what's right when no one is looking, because we're living for the betterment of the spirit of the world, not for a prize.

That approach is my faith in action. It lets me begin a new life every day.

+ + +

I try to live my life positively and on purpose. My watchwords are *awareness, accountability,* and *action*: I need to have my eyes looking up, not down at the little computer in my hand; I need to take accountability for my own energy; and I need always to be involved.

On the way to our destiny, we all deal with hardships, pitfalls, unfairness, trials. And because this is the same for everyone else on the planet, we should tread lightly.

But we mustn't be patsies. When people show us who

they are, we should believe them; we can choose to engage with them or not, but we need to believe them.

Who are we allowing to motivate and inspire us? Who has our ear? Is what they're saying positive or is it destructive? What and whom are we willing to release and let go of? We must invest in the power of goodbye—be willing to say, "That movie is no longer showing." Ditch the therapy sessions of trying to figure someone out. They are who they are. And we don't need to really care, in the end, what happened to them. Their history might explain *why* they are who they are, but it won't make us feel any better when we're treated poorly. We will never get those days, hours, years back. So don't waste time; it's fleeting.

Love isn't always a feeling. It's also an action. It's how we choose to treat people even if we don't like them. We should build people up when and where we can; but if there's no hope, say a blessing and move on—remember the blessings of boundaries. Write a letter, say a prayer, and then burn it.

The people who make a difference in this world are the people who love others. So we need to love those we don't like. We just shouldn't hang out with them.

+ + +

The most strategic way to let go of our past is to continually create a new present and thus a new future. But we can't be the best version of ourselves if we don't know who the hell we are. We need to find out, and quickly. And then be better at being whoever we find out we are.

As I keep saying, our energy is everything. If we find out we're afraid, we should try replacing fear with curiosity. If we don't like what we discover about ourselves, we should try replacing self-loathing with self-care.

Above all, we must appreciate our blessings. Take comedian Pete Holmes's words as a mantra: we *are* the traffic.

So let's all stop complaining.

◆ ◆ ◆

These last few years have represented, for so many of us, the intersection of grief and gratitude. For my family—well, we were starting to think about coming out of a pandemic when my mother was killed . . .

It's good to cry, but not forever, because there's always a new day. We can use our gratitude as a weapon against sorrow. Other weapons include integrity, forgiveness, service, showing up. And don't forget music, dance, art. Letting the day's own troubles be sufficient for the day. Matthew 6:34 bears repeating: "Therefore do not worry about tomorrow, for tomorrow will worry about its own things. Sufficient for the day is its own trouble."

There is seed time, and then there is harvest time. There are mountains and valleys. We can be grateful and be in pain at the same time. Some days, we might think, "Today I feel no hope. No faith. No joy." That's okay. It's the staying in the ditch that's not okay. So let's not deny the pain; let's just focus, too, on the good that's all around. We have only to set our energy toward it and—presto!—there it is.

Yes, I truly believe that, after everything.

◆ ◆ ◆

My grandmother had one fervent wish for all of us—that when we cross over, the first thing we hear will be the words of Matthew 25:23: "Well done, good and faithful servant."

There's nothing more important than character. Everything starts and ends with character. Even after you're gone, people will remember your character and what you stood for and how you made them feel in your presence.

My mother lived the life of a good and faithful servant. I believe she's heard those words spoken to her. Now it's my turn to live a life that ensures that I, too, hear those words one day.

If ever I'm tempted to think, "Why me? Why us? Why

the Avant family?" I quickly reverse that and think, "Why *not* me? It rains on the just and the unjust." Like so many people, I have a really hard time watching the news, because it's filled with tragedy. But believe me, once you feel tragedy yourself, you desperately want to know you're not alone, and you find other stories of grief oddly comforting. Why not all of us indeed?

I said to Ted a few months after Mom's death, "The thing is, Ted, the buck stops with me."

He looked quizzically at me. (This is not a rare event!)

"What I mean is, maybe that guy was going to keep doing what he was doing," I said. "He might have hurt other people. But my mother's shield was too strong for him; the buck stopped with her, just as the buck now stops with me, with us. She was always looking out for people; was always in service. Even on her last night. It's our job, now."

I also remember thinking, "Thank God I didn't just become an orphan overnight." After all, that happens to children around the world all the time in so many sad and various ways. People leave this planet every single day. At least I'd had more than five decades with my mother; at least I still had my father. I had more blessings than I could count. And no one lives forever.

There's a certain benefit to knowing that no one has an unlimited amount of time on this earth. For a start, it means that there's to be no wallowing in victimhood. Instead, I choose to commit to the magic of empathy. We can all do well by simply doing the next good thing.

We need to see everything as it really is. Accept that this is it for the moment. And then make a change based on the knowing and accepting of what is.

We humans often feel defeated, but we aren't.

We members of the Avant family aren't victims. We are the most blessed family imaginable.

You see, we had Jacqueline . . .

SWEET POTATO PIE

My mom knew something; I'm sure of it.

On a Monday late in the year 2021, I had been feeling weird all day, and then Tuesday we woke up to news of a mass shooting at Oxford High School in Michigan. "*This* is what the heaviness is," I thought. I couldn't believe that parents were going to have to go and identify their teenagers, right before Christmas, right after Thanksgiving. "My mom's not gonna be good about this," I thought, "because she's so sensitive about school shootings—they devastate her."

I called Mom at 4:45 p.m., but Dad said she was taking a nap.

My mom and I texted back and forth about a damn sweet potato pie, and that's when she wrote, "Think you'll be happy."

Then I went to sleep as if it were any old Tuesday night. But it wouldn't be any old Tuesday night.

On the way to the hospital later that night, I prayed for divine intelligence to work through everybody who was helping my mom—divine intelligence and divine wisdom. "Whoever is touching my mom, I pray that they know what they're doing," I whispered as I drove. Quickly, though, my prayer deepened into a pool of acceptance: "Whatever is the divine will for her life, so be it." Perhaps this is the central test of faith: even when faced with the worst, we have to stand in faith and let the divine will do as it may.

When I got to the hospital, I had no idea where to park—in fact, I was so confused that I parked in entirely the wrong place for where my mother had been taken.

When I got out of the car and realized my mistake, I walked around a bit, lost, scared. I eventually found a security guard and breathlessly told him where I needed to go.

There are angels everywhere; you just have to be open to recognizing them. Instead of sullenly pointing me in the right direction, as some might have, he actually left his post. He walked me to the correct elevator, rode with me, took me down to a different lobby, and walked me across to the correct building.

And then, as I left him, he simply said, "God bless you."

To this day, I'm not entirely sure he worked at Cedars—and I don't mean this in a joking way. His angelic presence reminded me of the moment in scripture when Mary Magdalene goes to the tomb to minister to the body of Jesus, but she is met by an angel who instructs her that Jesus has risen. That hospital guard seemed of another world altogether. He was another Clarence Odbody.

When I found the proper waiting room, and my father and my brother, I started to ask questions about what the fuck had happened. I think the delayed shock had finally hit me.

My father said, "Stop cursing, Nicole."

It was then I noticed that my father's left sock had blood on it.

"What the hell is going on?" I demanded.

"I don't know," my father said. "I heard sirens; there was a commotion. It all woke me. I walked down the hallway and found your mom on the floor. She was breathing heavily. I guess I switched places with the security guard who was kind of holding her up. Then I was outside, and it was freezing. I had my pajamas on."

A moment passed. "I didn't get to put on my robe," he added.

Another long moment. "I didn't know what was happening. I still don't."

Epilogue

Clarence

As I mentioned in an earlier chapter, the second night after my mom died, a group of childhood friends came over to share stories and to bring love. Among them were Lisa, my best friend since the fourth grade, and many friends from kindergarten. They'd known my parents almost all their lives. I was amazed at how many of those friends now described my mom as their superhero; she had given them so much, just as she'd given me. (You can see what she meant to people by the extracts from some of the notes I received that I included at the beginning of each chapter of this book.)

That night, my dad sat with us; all these friends of mine encircled him, surrounding him with love, sharing stories of my mom.

As I watched him there, I felt terribly sad for him, but I was also filled with a deep gratitude. For the past few months, I'd been thanking my father for making a different choice than the one *his* father made. My dad stayed around for me and my brother; he was committed to our lives. He made that choice; he didn't do what so many others have done. And it has made all the difference.

These days, Dad isn't so sure on his feet—he's in his early nineties, after all!—but he's still incredibly independent, and I want to respect that. So each morning, when he heads upstairs to take his shower, I sneak up after him, wait to hear the water running, then remain outside the bathroom with my cup of tea, listening to make sure he doesn't fall. Just as he's never had to spend another night in his house since December 1, 2021—he came straight from the hospital to my house, and he hasn't left—so I've also never left his side since. Each morning as I listen to him take his shower, I know, somewhere deep down, that even though I couldn't save my mother, that won't stop me from trying to save my father just as long as I can.

Dad would gain particular comfort after the death of my mom from a visit from the children of his own closest friends—Kidada, Rashida, Casey, and Nicole. In fact, that comfort was profound for him, in ways that I would never have expected. Again we all shared stories, compared and relished memories.

Why we didn't do this when my mom was still alive . . .

well, we did not, and there's nothing to be done about that now. But I swear she was there. You could see her reflected in the eyes of my friends, in the way they honored Mom by recounting stories of her kindness, her quirks, her love, her laughter. And you could see her, too, in my father's eyes, in the etched lines on his hands, a love undimmed by loss, alive and sparkling still in the memory of Jacqueline Avant, my mom.

We can't banish evil.

We can't hide from misery.

We all inevitably endure trauma and pain.

So how do we go on, move forward?

We have to learn to swim through trauma so that we don't drown; we have to live—and live fully—for all of those who can't.

We must always choose the joy.

Choose to swim. Choose to not go down with the ship.

Acknowledgments

The brief quotes at the start of chapters 2 through 10 are taken from hundreds of beautiful notes my family received after the loss of my mother. Thank you to everyone for sharing your beautiful sentiments about my mother.

The Avant-Sarandos family has been supported and loved through our terrible trauma by so many people—too many, in fact, to mention. I apologize that I can't name everyone—to do so would need another book-length publication. But I would very much like to make mention of the following people:

To the other "first responders" on December 1: Gwyneth, Amy, Candace, Danielle, Irena, Laura, Colleen, and Juliet. Thank you for never asking—but always knowing—what I needed and when I needed it.

To Colleen, thank you for our five-to-seven-hour crab dinners that have sustained me spiritually, emotionally, and physically.

To Juliet—thank you for making sure I always had my delicious homemade minestrone soup that always warmed my soul and thank you for always thinking of Clarence.

Acknowledgments

Who knew that a gingerbread house would bring so much joy to his heart?

To Candace: thank you for EVERYTHING!

To Debbie: Thank you for always capturing and documenting our special memories through your wonderful photographs.

To my wonderful friends who checked in on day one and often and helped keep me afloat with beautiful cards and sentiments: Bobby and Malissa, Jessica and Jerry, Patty, Sheryl and Rob, Halle, Eve, Jeff and John, Maureen, Cornelia, Susana, Leo, Vivi, Naomi, Amy and John, Haydn, Michael and James, Pharrell and Helen, Tracey E., Tracey K., Lori, Marilyn, Mellody, Meghan, Jennifer S., Darnell, Bishop Jakes, Richard B., Giselle, Susie, Kelly, Lyndie, Roma and Mark, Arseni, Georgie and Melissa, Rick and Tina, John R., Ben and Amelie, Scott and Molly, Eden, Jennifer, Amanda and Jason, Sean and Scottie, Reese, Molly and Jimmy, Courtney, Mitch and Mary Jo, Ricky and Jane, Will A., Kevin H., Bobby K., Veronica and Brian, Ellen and Portia, Kim K., Harley and Daniel, Adam and Jackie, Chrisette and Reggie, Herb, Nyakio, Susan F., Holly and Rodney, LLJ, L.T., Penny, Mikey and Jay, Adam S., Kidada, Rashida, Tina, QDIII, Nicole R., Cheryl and Haim, Tamar and Bob, Tania and Fares, HFJ and Emily, Crystal and Ray, Brian

M., Thelma, Mayor Adams, Guy S., Christian, Jessica and Cash, Nina and Frank, Anne S., Michael E., Michael M., Michael B., Chad B., Chaz and Karen.

To my extended family:

Aunt Jean, Aunt Anne, Brian, Richie, Dawn, Vicky, Angie, Elgin, Douglas, and Madeline, and to my fabulous godmothers, Audrey and Gail: thank you all for every text, phone call, and email, filled as they were, with such love, care, and concern.

To the truth tellers who helped me get this book to the publisher on time: Oprah Winfrey, Arianna Huffington, Cleo Wade, and Jay Shetty. Thank you! Thank you! Thank you!

To my friend DVF, who offered to be my mom when I needed one and who reminded me that the best way to honor my mom was to *live my life to the fullest*.

To Maria, who wrote me the most beautiful, grounding, and healing emails that helped get me through the night.

To the "young couple" GP and Brad: thank you and your children for loving Clarence and making his heart smile again.

To my mother's friends who checked in on me often and who helped put together so many missing pieces: Adrienne, Elaine, Sue, Lynne, Janet, Carolyn, Lenore, Tina, Phoebe,

Acknowledgments

Audrey and Gail, Mattie, Donnie, Amy, and Esta-Anne.

Thank you to Irena, and to everyone who made sure that my family was fed for months!

Thank you, Jen, for the gluten-free lasagna; thank you, Cleo, for the casserole bursting with gluten; thank you, Colleen, for the much needed and desired fried chicken; thank you, George, for the tequila; thank you, Bruce and Bryan, for the whacky flavored ice cream; and a huge thank-you to the following people for constantly making sure that we had everything we needed or craved at all times: Lynda and Stewart, Wendy, Bui and Herb, Shelli and Irving, Dale and Gloria, Dora and Danielle, Julie and Donnie, Tom and Monique, Nadine and Fred, Lynne and Norman, Florence and Harry, Jon and Laurie, Lysa and Grant, Chrisette and Reggie, Gelila and Wolfgang, Sybil and Matthew, Olivier and Zoe, Cheryl and Haim, Tania and Bob, Danielle and Reinout, Tania and Fares.

To Charlie Rivkin: thank you for dreaming a wonderful dream for me and making sure that I woke up to it.

Thank you, Justin, Eric, and Holly, for the gorgeous florals that brightened up our home and our souls.

Thank you, Elgin Charles and Damone Roberts, for always making sure I looked my best even when I felt my worst.

Thank you, my dear godfather, Quincy Jones, for coming

to the rescue per usual and for being so devoted to Clarence's well-being. Your wonderful idea of a Tuesday-night dinner ritual helps keep us all sane.

Thank you to all my father's friends who made sure to visit and/or check in constantly and love him deeply, even if from afar.

Al Haymon, Barack and Michelle Obama, Oprah Winfrey, Tyler Perry, Gayle King, Queen Latifah, Reggie Hudlin, Jon and Angie Platt, Berry Gordy, Irving and Shelli Azoff, Mai and James Lassiter, Nina and Frank Cooper, Audrey Smaltz and Gail Marquis, Brenda Andrews, Lionel Richie, Debra Lee, Julius Hollis, Brenda Richie, Richard Baskin, David Geffen, Alan Grubman, Andrew Young, Danny Bakewell, Ron Sweeny, Guy Abrahams, Gwen Adolf, Dr. Keith Black, Benny Medina, L.A. and Erica Reid, Jimmy Jam and Lisa Harris, Terry and Indira Lewis, Jerry and Tina Moss, Abe and Annika Somer, Phil Q., Casey Wasserman, Lucien and Caroline Grange, Dolores Robinson, Jeff Harlston, Zach Horowitz, Don Passman, Gene Salomon, Clive and Patty Fox, Susanne de Passé, Smokey Robinson, Howlie Davis, Julius Hollis, "Chad the Chad," Magic and Cookie Johnson, Ron Burkle, LaTanya and Sam Jackson, Cathy Hughes, Michael and Mattie Lawson, Lou and Page Adler, Norman Nixon and Debbie Allen, Jolene and George Schlatter, Joseph and Tina Porter.

Acknowledgments

Thank you, Tina Stephens, for the numerous Xian dinners and music videos that put Clarence in a happy place.

Thank you, Neil and David, for your time and efforts and helping us put our family home *in order*. I am eternally grateful.

Thank you, Jon Platt, for going above and beyond for Clarence in every way.

Thank you to Pepe and everyone at the Polo Lounge for making sure that Mr. Avant always felt right at home when he made his way back to the hotel.

Thank you, Craig Susser, and everyone at Craig's, for loving my parents and taking such great care of them on their date nights.

Thank you, Gabe, and everyone at the Tower Bar for the fun and happy nights with my parents and the Smiths.

Thank you, Silvio and Eddie and everyone at Il Piccolino, for treating my parents like a king and queen.

Thank you, Jonah, for always reminding me to stay "prayed up" and for making sure that I always have my stationery ready so I could keep up with my thank-you notes.

Thank you, Michael and Lydia, for being such great friends and for hosting wonderful dinners that give me a reason to leave my house and have a life.

Thank you, Bill Maher, Chris Rock, Jerry Seinfeld,

Sebastian Maniscalco, and Dave Chappelle for bringing laughter back to my soul.

To my Full Moon Sisters: Jen and Amanda. Thank you for keeping me sane, making me laugh, and filling my heart with love and laughter, especially during an eclipse or a retrograde.

Thank you to my Shiva Tribe: Gwyneth, Brigette, Laura, Colleen, Juliet, Daun, Lisa, Sara, Jennifer, Monique, Cleo, and Shannon. I'm so grateful for your friendship, love, prayers, and support.

To my NoCo gals: Katy, Sheryl, Whitney, and Cameron. Thank you for the long and warm hugs, spiritual wisdom, and much needed silliness.

Thank you to all my friends from nursery school, Hawthorne Elementary, and Beverly Hills High School, who have been showing up for me since 1971: Cece, Ross, Dominique, Anthony, Laura, Katherine, Lisa, Todd, Gregg, Michele, Jon, Stacey, Paige, Steve, David, Peter, Angella, Greg, Albert, Carrie, Jill, Suzanne, Jennifer, Victor, Steven, Berry, Howard, Oren, Darren, and many more!

Thank you to all of my childhood, high school, and college teachers and professors for constantly challenging me and pushing me to expand my mind and open my heart.

My Island friends: Amb. Rood, Andy, India and David,

Amanda, Rebecca, Kika, Michael, Juan, Sibilla, Micheline, John, Haideh, Jacqueline and Jean-Charles, Pierre, Mavis, Reuben, and June.

Thank you to the Vision Queen, Aleen Keshishian, for "seeing" this entire journey at our casual dinner at the Tower Bar in 2019. I'm so grateful for your insights and support and your crazy "before and after" texts in the middle of the night.

Thank you to my manager, Zack Morgenroth, for *always* taking my calls even when you don't want to and for always having the best advice for every question I present to you. Your patience is the greatest gift, and I'm eternally grateful for everything that you do for me.

Thank you to my publicists: Katie Greenthal and Matthew Avento. I'm so grateful to you for your thinking-out-of-the-box style, smart ideas, guidance, patience, and truth.

To Mary: I'm grateful for all—especially the eye roll emojis regarding my IG questions that have me on the floor laughing every day.

Thank you to Luom Cooper for helping me get all areas of my life in order.

To my everyday angels: Evelyn and Andy. Thank you for always showing up when I need you.

Thank you, Jan Miller, for understanding and appreciating my family, our history, and my story. Thank you for

Acknowledgments

being a wonderful literary agent, champion, and friend. And many thanks to Ali, too.

Thank you, Judith Curr, Daniella Wexler, Ghjulia Romiti, and Paul Olsewski. I'm so grateful to you for your notes, suggestions, and ideas, and for guiding me through this process. And a huge thank-you to everyone at HarperOne for your guidance and support.

Thank you to everyone who sent cards and flowers and made donations to my mother's favorite causes.

A very special thank-you to Beverly Hills police chief Mark Stainbrook and the Beverly Hills Police Department, Beverly Hills Fire Department and Paramedics, Los Angeles Police Department/Hollywood Division, attorney Shawn Holley, Mayor Lili Bosse, and Los Angeles deputy district attorney Victor Avila for their unwavering dedication to public service and for your daily service and commitment to the community.

To my family: Clarence, Alex and Airess, Sarah, Tony, Diesel, and Luca—you are my everything, everyday.

To Teddy: you are my absolute favorite human on the planet, and I thank you for being you. Your kind heart, sense of humor, and thoughtfulness are unmatched.

About the Author

Nicole Avant is a philanthropist, filmmaker, and former diplomat. After a career in entertainment and political fundraising, she served as the United States ambassador to the Bahamas under President Obama. She has produced the critically acclaimed documentaries *The Black Godfather* and *Trees of Peace*, and *Six Triple Eight*, a Tyler Perry movie about an all-female, all-Black battalion in World War II. She lives in Los Angeles with her husband, Ted; her ninety-two-year-old father, Clarence; and their dogs.